WONDERHUNT

a scavenger hunt for the weary soul

a scavenger hunt for the weary soul

WONDERHUNT: A SCAVENGER HUNT FOR THE WEARY SOUL

Copyright © 2022 Kim Kotecki. All rights reserved. Cover and book design by Jason Kotecki. Printed in Canada. No part of this book may be reproduced in any form or by any means—whether electronic, digital, mechanical, or otherwise—without permission in writing from the publisher, except by a reviewer, who may quote brief passages in a review.

Contact JBiRD iNK, Ltd., PO Box 943, Sheboygan, WI 53082.

Unless otherwise noted, Scripture quotations are taken from the New American Standard Bible® (NASB). Copyright © 1960, 1962, 1963, 1968, 1971, 1972, 1973, 1975, 1977, 1995 by The Lockman Foundation. Used by permission. www.Lockman.org.

Scriptures marked NLT are taken from the Holy Bible, New Living Translation. Copyright © 1996, 2004, 2015 by Tyndale House Foundation. Used by permission of Tyndale House Ministries, Carol Stream, Illinois 60188. All rights reserved.

Library of Congress Control Number: 2022944894
ISBN: 978-0-9850732-4-4 (softcover)
ISBN: 978-0-9850732-5-1 (ebook)

Books may be purchased for educational, business, or promotional use. For information on bulk purchases, please contact our team at 1-608-554-0803, or email store@escapeadulthood.com.

First Paperback Edition: October 2022
10 9 8 7 6 5 4 3 2 1

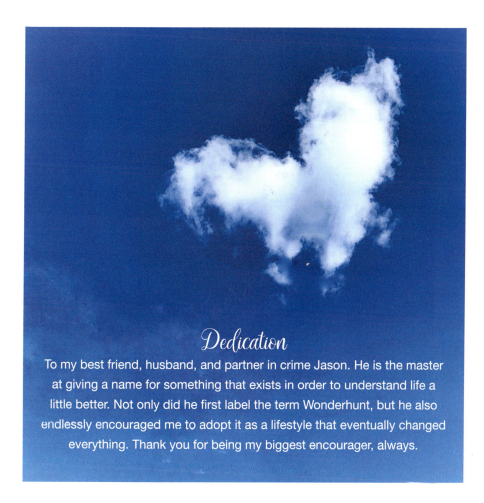

Dedication

To my best friend, husband, and partner in crime Jason. He is the master at giving a name for something that exists in order to understand life a little better. Not only did he first label the term Wonderhunt, but he also endlessly encouraged me to adopt it as a lifestyle that eventually changed everything. Thank you for being my biggest encourager, always.

Table of Contents

Introduction 11

Chapter 1: Come at Me, Bro! 21

Chapter 2: My Joyful Haul. 33

Chapter 3: Way Back When 49

Chapter 4: It's Time to Wonderhunt 59

31 Challenges

Challenge 1: Wholehearted Living. 71

Challenge 2: Sunny-Side Up. 75

Challenge 3: A Bit of Silliness 79

Challenge 4: Courageous Color 83

Challenge 5: Surprise Yourself 87

Challenge 6: Reroute with Grace 91

Challenge 7: Seeing Sepia 95

Challenge 8: Reclaim Joy 99

Challenge 9: Nothing to See Here. 103

Challenge 10: Facing the Day 107

Challenge 11: Where's Whimsy?. 111

Challenge 12: See with New Eyes. 115

Challenge 13: Life's Love Letter 119

Challenge 14: Thrill of the Chase 123

Challenge 15: Mirror, Mirror. 127

Challenge 16: Wild Child	131
Challenge 17: The Making of a Moment	135
Challenge 18: Winning at Twinning	139
Challenge 19: Looking Up	143
Challenge 20: Proof of Life	147
Challenge 21: Blessed Are the Creative	151
Challenge 22: Going Undercover	155
Challenge 23: Honey, I Shrunk Myself	159
Challenge 24: Eggscellent	163
Challenge 25: Window Wonder	167
Challenge 26: Surprise Me	171
Challenge 27: Gray vs. Green	175
Challenge 28: Object of My Affection	179
Challenge 29: Friendly Neighborhood Animals	183
Challenge 30: Watch Out	187
Challenge 31: Hopeful Healing	191
Conclusion: Part 1	197
Conclusion: Part 2	209
Acknowledgments	229
About the Author	233
Fellow Wonderhunters	234

INTRODUCTION

Suzy had a peaceful voice. I anticipated hearing her sing each morning and throughout the day. I adored her and her tiny blue-painted house. She zipped in and out of her pint-sized castle hundreds of times a day.

Suzy was a wren, my wren (although my sister, Kristy, might say the same thing). I have a faint memory of my mom naming her from our kitchen window where we enjoyed watching her backyard shenanigans. Suzy and I shared countless hours together in the shade of a decades-old oak tree on Shady Lane. She'd sit on her perch above me, and I'd swing back and forth on the white wooden seat, listening to her chirp and sing. I always imagined some of her songs were specifically for me.

Suzy is my first memory of wonder.

Memories that last decades have strong sensory components, don't they? My memories of Suzy sure do. I can still hear her sweet, whimsical music—the soundtrack of my '80s childhood. To this day, the sound of singing birds brings me back to this simpler time.

These early memories also contain the epic smells of summertime in the Midwest, which were generated from a playful mix of oak and maple leaves and the unmatched scent of freshly cut grass. This magical combination of outside smells will forever whisk me back to seven-year-old Kim Halm. My straight blonde hair was cut short, and my long legs (always covered in bruises) were lankier than the other girls in my second-grade class at St. Patrick's School. I didn't mind though. I liked being tall like my three older sisters. Any chance I could find to be like one of my K-Mart Sisters (as we were called), I'd jump at it. Yep, my parents went with all Ks: Karen, Kathi, Kristy, and the caboose (as my mom still calls me)—Kim.

We all have treasured, wonder-filled moments that populate our memory banks. The big ones get a lot of fanfare, sometimes even video footage. Wonder is easily found in the Hallmark-card occasions, like the birth of a baby or the magical exchange of wedding vows. But you and I both know that wonder is also found in simple, everyday moments. All we have to do is to make an effort to notice.

That's what Wonderhunt is all about, Charlie Brown . . . noticing. Seems simple enough, but it's not easy. It requires disciplined intention, and most days we're too busy to notice the wonder all around us.

Not surprisingly, nature is still my happy place. It offers me a quick route to de-stress and think clearly. Even now, as I sit here on this chilly day, I'm drawn to the wonder just outside my window. I see a playful chickadee hopping on a branch nearby and a pair of peaceful deer sleeping. Lifting my head a little higher, I notice lines in the lake, gently moving from the lapping water. And the pine trees are casting long shadows from the midmorning sun, leaning together with the same exact slant, like dancers in synch at a hip-hop concert.

Wonder is here, whether I take the time to notice or not. Noticing is where the power lies!

Wonder is not only available to you right now; wonder is always waiting for you.

If you lift your head for just a moment, you will experience wonder. Don't overthink it; just give it a try and see what happens. (Go ahead! I'll play the predictable *Jeopardy* theme song in my head and wait for you.)

You did it. High five!

What wonder did you experience? How did it surprise you?

My imagination is racing with all of the possibilities of the wonder you just experienced. Was it something visual, such as a shadow or an image inviting strong emotions? Or maybe it was a sound that caught your attention? It could have been the feel of your chest rising and falling from a deep breath of air. Wonder is in *all* of it!

Thanks for playing along with me. Getting involved and treating the Wonderhunt journey like stepping-stones in a mossy, enchanted forest will be an important mindset to have in building excitement for what this process will lead you to. My hope is that Wonderhunt will not just remain a theory or a fleeting idea, but instead will inspire you into action.

Wonder has become a powerful portal for me, a time machine to the childhood self that still exists within my soul. Seven-year-old Kim had a spunk to her, and boy do I miss her spirit. Activating wonder reawakens this younger version of me, the girl who believes in the impossible—without the distractions of self-doubt, fear, and lies.

And, much to my delight, wonder has become a gateway back to my childlike faith. When I experience wonder, I see the face of God, and I hear him say, "I am here. Do you see me? I see you, and I love you."

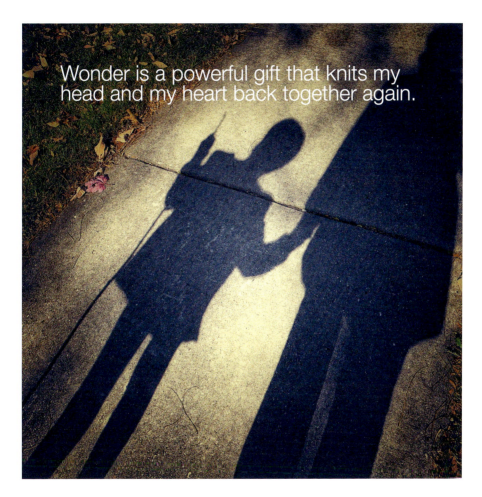
Wonder is a powerful gift that knits my head and my heart back together again.

What does wonder do for your spirit?

Amidst the division and hurt found in our world today, the gift of wonder is for everyone. It's a universal language and exists free of judgement. It's diverse, inclusive, and equal. It's not reserved for a certain age group or those in attendance at any particular church, temple, mosque, or school of thought. No matter what your relationship or experiences have been and currently are regarding faith, spirituality, and religion, wonder coexists in *all* of it.

Fair warning, though, and I am speaking from personal experience: When you start to open your eyes new to wonder, watch out! Surprises await and generously bring lessons for living your best life. It's a wild ride! If this sounds like something you're seeking, then woo-hoo! You're in the right place!

Going back to my first memory of wonder—my feathered friend, Suzy—I think about how her sweet songs filled my childhood with peace and joy. Memories of these moments continue to bless my life. My prayer for you as we start this Wonderhunt journey together is that your efforts to reawaken wonder will serve as encouragement and inspire you to see your life with new eyes.

Are there any connections between your first memories of wonder and how you experience wonder as an adult?

CHAPTER 1

Come at Me, Bro!

My feet were cold, but I wasn't complaining. It felt nice, refreshing even. It was magic hour. As I walked deeper into the woods, my senses awoke and finally, after days of needing it, I took a deep breath. Cold air rushed into my lungs— just in time.

It was exhilarating, freeing, healing.

In that moment, on that path, something *big* was beginning. I lifted my head for the first time in far too long. My focus shifted away from all of the needs of those around me, and I started to open my eyes and notice the present moment. Simple surprises started to unlock my heart.

I saw the bare trees. But instead of being disappointed that they were missing their beautiful red and yellow fall colors, I realized how much unexpected beauty they possessed, silhouetted in the low light. I couldn't get enough. I was drinking it in, filling my soul with peace.

Their lack of color somehow reminded me of my own heart, and this metaphor hit me hard.

As the sun lowered in slow motion, the pace of my breathing followed, and I noticed I was smiling. Deep, generous, soul-filling breaths were flooding my lungs now, like an inflating hot-air balloon preparing for its maiden voyage. This was, indeed, my new beginning. With fresh air reopening my lungs, I noticed the sun was sitting upon the horizon, glowing with a gentle grace. Time stood still long enough for me to notice.

The light filled my heart with hope, and in this simple moment, my soul rediscovered wonder.

I felt seen.
I felt loved.

On this particular afternoon in December, I found myself in a challenging zone that led me to take that desperate walk. We were coming to the end of a marathon of a year with the finale featuring a crash landing of birthday madness. All three of our kids celebrate their special days in a twenty-day spread, and with Christmas just six days later, I was drowning in a fog of overwhelm. Jason was states away inspiring mental health professionals at his last speaking event of the year—a gift and a privilege we don't take lightly in our work together.

Amidst all of our blessings, my life had become a blur. I didn't have a free minute to think clearly. Although being in survival mode had become a familiar reality the last several years, I had grown sick of this state of being.

You know the commonly used self-care metaphor of your cup being full or empty? Well, my cup was neither full nor empty. My poor cup got thrown out the window by our youngest daughter while I was trying to sneak in a five-minute shower. (Moms, you know the drill: soap and hair only, no shaving.)

I hadn't taken a deep breath in days.

My sweet parents were visiting during Jason's trip and were eager to help. Let's be honest though: the deer-in-headlights look on their faces was legit when I told (didn't ask) them that I was going to sneak out for a bit.

"But, it's almost dark," Mom pointed out in a shaky, semi-panicked voice.

I knew they felt my stress, which left me sad (and embarrassed). They were right to wonder if I would return. Lucy, our six-year-old (with a sweet old soul) would talk their ears off the entire time. Our middleman, three-year-old Ben, was a *very* big fan of having his mom *in* the house and *not* on a walk. The biggest challenge, though, would certainly be our almost one-year-old, Ginny Rose. You should not take your eye off of her for a second, lest she double-fist permanent markers and color the entire house, including her own face (and Ben's sweet, round face too).

Still, my parents let me walk out the door. That is true love. I owe you big, Mom and Dad!

My official job title here at Escape Adulthood is Little Miss Details, which makes me smile as I think about those silly books from my childhood by Roger Hargreaves. Think "Director of Operations" meets "Executive Assistant" meets "Household Manager" meets "Homeschool Mom" meets "Taxi Driver," etc. — times one hundred.

Yes, it's a superpower of mine to manage the minutia. As a former kindergarten teacher, having a handle on the chaos (with a smile on my face) was critical. You'd get eaten alive by the five-year-olds (or maybe more so the parents) if you didn't have five different things planned before morning recess. But like all gifts, time and chaos management are simultaneously my greatest strengths and my greatest weaknesses.

On good days I'm juggling the balls in this three-ring circus with one hand tied behind my back, making it look as easy as Michael Jordan winning all of those championships in the '90s. However, on my not-so-good days, I'm stricken by the effects of my kryptonite: OVERWHELM (in all caps, all the time). For some reason, I stop taking deep breaths of air (not great, Bob!). This shallow-breathing condition can go on for days. Any little thing can set me off, resulting in one of two predictable outcomes: crying ("I can't do it anymore!") or anger ("Come at me, bro!"). Unhealthy and off-balance, I know. Sorry, family! I now have better coping strategies, which is what this book is all about, so stick with me.

In the woods, standing on that path, I noticed my heart was bare, just like the trees. I had nothing left to give. Zero. I was giving all that I had to my awesome kiddos; my husband, whom I adore; our shared work, which I treasure; and our beloved community of Adultitis Fighters. All good things.

It was a season of constant serving, and as much as I loved it all, it was a lot. I knew that I was too serious most of the time (which I disliked about myself), and little by little, I had lost an important part of my core being: the childlike, wonder-loving girl under the oak tree on Shady Lane. Remember her? I barely did.

With the sun sitting on the horizon, I took a selfie. I'm so glad I did because rarely in life do you get a photo of such a defining moment. This picture records my breakthrough—the exact point in which my head and my heart reconnected in a way that changed *everything.*

SHIP DATE
Nov 11, 2022

Packing slip 83692917-36537936

SHIP TO
Margo Petro
53 academy ave
Apt 101
Pittsburgh, Pennsylvania 15228
United States
(201) 874-7127

RETURN ADDRESS
Escape Adulthood
11201 Ed Brown Rd, Unit A
Charlotte, North Carolina 28273
United States
608-554-0803
store@escapeadulthood.com

Your order of Nov 11, 2022 — Order ID 12131

Product	Qty
Wonderhunt Book - 1+	1

Thanks for your order! Remember, everything you order from Escape Adulthood is guaranteed to be 100% Adultitis-free.

Sign up for free Adultitis-fighting tips and inspiration at EscapeAdulthood.com/subscribe.

On this walk, I heard whispers in my heart; it was a loving and compassionate invitation to heal and grow. Somehow, I knew immediately what God was asking me to do next. It seemed too simple. I felt called to come back to this place again by myself—and soon. There were lessons for me here. This clarity of thought was like a long-awaited glass of lemonade after days and days out in the heat.

My reality was about to change, and I was ready.

Turns out this magical trail was only two minutes from our house and right on the edge of a nearby lake. It wasn't stroller-friendly, which means I hadn't spent any time there in the five years we'd lived on this side of town. Within minutes, I could find myself on the tree-lined path—which would soon serve as a welcoming yellow-brick road back to my soul—one hopeful step at a time. I made a promise in my heart that I would accept the invitation for more of this wonder.

I flew back home as joyful as Suzy the shenanigating wren, seeing everything with new eyes along the way. And to my surprise, when I walked through the front door and saw all three kiddos huddled together on the couch waiting for me (and my nervous parents looking out the window), I didn't feel suffocated by their overeager state. For the first time in a long time, I appreciated the beauty of this season. I knew with confidence I was right where I needed to be. No resentment or overwhelm, no tears or anger. Just peace and joy. Wow, what a surprising gift.

In my desperate moment, God used wonder to get my attention. This was the start of a new season of growth and self-discovery, one that would be inspired, intentional, and filled with possibilities beyond my wildest imagination.

Maybe you are finding yourself in a challenging season of survival-based living right now?

Are you weary?

Are your heart and head disconnected and in need of a restart?

Are you longing for a path back to yourself so you can experience inspired living?

If so, you're not alone. In fact, you're in good company. It happens to the best of us for all sorts of reasons and in varying seasons.

Grab my hand. I've been right where you are, and I have good news.

It's magic hour! The sun is shining bright on the horizon, and the path ahead of us is filled with all the things our souls need to shine—extraordinary gifts found in ordinary places.

Get ready for a hopeful journey ahead. Wonder is waiting.

Come at me, bro!

CHAPTER 2

My Joyful Haul

I was sixteen years young the night I met Jason. He likes to tell the story about how he'll never forget what I was wearing that December evening. Let's go top to bottom, starting with a Santa hat, Rudolph the Red-Nosed Reindeer boxer shorts, bright-red tights, and black combat boots. Hey, don't judge, it was 1994, so this was just about right. (Or maybe it was just me?)

We were two of about twenty squirrely teenagers from a Christian retreat program gathered together for a social outing: Christmas caroling! Jason was the older college guy with the sweet smile. I liked his vibe (and he was cute). He was witty, thoughtful, and deep. Oh, and I had heard he was a killer good artist, too, according to our mutual friend, Teresa (yes, we said "killer good" in the '90s).

His first words to me were, "So, you're the famous Kim Halm I've heard so much about." *Ha-ha!* It appeared Teresa had been talking to him about me also.

Although it would take us a few weeks until we started dating, it was only a few months before we knew this was "it." On the Christmas ornament I gave him our first holiday season together, I had it engraved with "the first of forever." When you know, you know.

After dating five years, we got married a solid seven days after I graduated college. We were beyond excited to finally start our lives together. We moved to a new city knowing no one and immediately founded what is now Escape Adulthood.

As a kid-loving kindergarten teacher and an artist creating a comic strip honoring childhood (based on the two of us), we were following a strong call in our hearts to rediscover our own childlike spirits and to help others do the same. Back then, we used the phrase "Return to Childhood." We were committed to this hope-filled perspective of living our lives with adventure, meaning, and joy, just like kids do naturally.

A few years in, we discovered and identified the widespread disease called Adultitis. We started to see it in our own lives as we became official "responsible adults." We lived on a tight budget, supported by my teaching salary. Jason worked all day on our hope-fueled venture. As we continued to invest in our baby business, debt grew quick (thank you, Aldi's, we couldn't have built this dream without your thirty-nine-cent canned veggies) and so did Adultitis.

Adultitis. Even if this is your first time hearing about this sneaky disease, I suspect you can guess what it's capable of. It has the ability to leave one jaded, distracted, and cynical. Quite literally, it means the "swelling of the adult." And too much adult brings about a slew of problems. Hearts become disconnected and distant. We find ourselves at risk of living "lives of quiet desperation," as Henry David Thoreau so accurately put it.

Adulting is no joke. We carry the weight, uncertainties, and insecurities brought on by everyday hardships. The buffet of challenges is endless: illness, relationships, money, chores, work stress, political strife, war, natural disasters, tragedies, and (a new one to all of us) a never-ending pandemic. Most of us admit to being over-committed and overwhelmed in thought and worry, distracted by all of it (and our phones) most of the time. And when we finally are convinced to use vacation time, we end up needing vacations from our vacations. Let's face it, most people stink at adulting. We knew what problem we wanted to solve; we just weren't sure how to decode it.

Fourteen years before that wonder-filled walk in the woods, Jason and I were in builder-mode as young entrepreneurs. We knew little about how to create or maintain a profitable business. With the support of very dear and generous friends and our two sets of parents always cheerleading from the sidelines, we spent almost ten years throwing a ton of spaghetti at walls to see what would stick.

Spoiler alert: not much stuck for a long time.

Our dreams were clear and fuzzy at the same time. This kept us humble and on our knees in prayer every single day for direction. We felt confident that we were following the call God had placed in our hearts, which required leaps of faith along the way, including me eventually quitting my safe and steady teaching job to dedicate all of my focus to this shared venture. Goodbye security (and insurance)! Some of the risks didn't pan out the way we had hoped. We learned a lot of lessons the hard way, like the time we made a total of $8.20 at a two-day craft fair in Milwaukee that had a $300 entry fee. That was a character-building weekend (wink). Building this business was proving to be hard, often discouraging work.

Quickly outgrowing our apartment, we'd joke with visitors that it was like living in a Hallmark store, except with a smoking section! Remember those from restaurants? The neighborhood smokers hung out outside our windows. We'd laugh with them and cry later. (Did I mention it was a long and tough season?)

Our reality became more challenging when our friends and siblings started building beautiful homes and having adorable babies. Tempted to abandon the dream altogether, we opted to persist, digging deeper into our own foundation of faith. We kept our heads down, building, visioning, and praying (while the mounds of debt and doubts loomed in the background).

Are we crazy? Is this even going to work? Will we have regrets if we quit too soon? Will we have our college loans paid off before we're fifty? Will we ever be able to convince a bank to give us a mortgage? Will we be able to start a family before it's too late? All these thoughts and more raced through our minds constantly.

Turns out, the answer to all of these questions was yes, but it would take time. Year after year, we prayed for more stability. Looking back, it's obvious to see how God provided what we needed next along the way and gave us the assurance that there was more than what we could see in front of us. We were given one arrow at a time. It was a foundational season of growth for us as young adults, as a newly married couple, and as small business owners. Lots of character was built, and our faith muscles grew stronger each year as we witnessed God opening doors we could never have opened on our own.

Eventually, as a solid business model started to take shape, we felt a nudge from heaven that it was time to also start building our family. *What? Is this responsible?* we wondered. It would be another leap of faith.

What happened next may be a familiar story for some. We stepped out in faith, growing ever more excited about this new adventure to start a family, only to be met with . . . crickets.

Jason and I were confused. Had we gotten the wires crossed? It sure seemed like God had asked us to prepare our hearts for a little one. We wanted to be parents. Hurt and fearful, three months turned into six, then twelve. Eighteen months and . . . nothing. It was a vulnerable and difficult time for both of us.

All the while, we kept busy working on our passion, and our business became more stable each month. In retrospect, it makes sense to see what God was doing—firming up our foundation for more growth.

When we finally learned I was pregnant, we were in a much more reliable position financially. Lucy Ruth entered our world and everything changed. Almost to the day, three years later, our chill middleman, Benjamin Walter, arrived. Then two years later Virginia Rose made her rapid-fire entrance, showing up two minutes after the midwives arrived in the middle of the night. Jason could now add something to his resume: artist, speaker, author, and *apprentice midwife.*

Boom. Just like that, we crammed a third car seat into the backseat and the adventure continued.

What had just happened? It was a whirlwind of blessings, and we treasured this family that felt as if it was assembled overnight. Because we weren't sure for a while if we'd become parents, we found ourselves appreciating it all with such intention, which informed our work and mission even more. We were grateful for this season of crazy chaos!

Jason and I spent a lot of effort managing the delicate balance. Working from home, traveling as a family to his speaking engagements (Lucy was on thirty-four

flights in her first year!), figuring out solo-parenting when he traveled—all while trying to be emotionally present to savor the many wonders of those first few years was . . . a lot.

We were work-at-home/homeschooling parents for twelve years before the pandemic required this of families all over the world during those handful of weeks that turned into months. In March of 2020, when the world was freaking out about the impossibility of this balance, Jason and I realized we had spent the last decade figuring out this exact puzzle with beautiful results. (High five, honey!) It happened to be one of our many "Corona Blessings" and one less thing for us to manage when the pandemic hit, allowing us to serve in ways we never imagined possible.

I now look back and fondly call this season my "joyful haul."

One minute I'd be reading bedtime stories with funny voices, and the next minute I was creating a proposal for a speaking client so we could pay for eight straight years of diapers. Holy sleep deprivation, Batman!

As a thirty-five-year-old introvert who spent the first decade of her adult life with a well-established morning routine of prayer and exercise, this flow of survival eventually left me feeling distant from myself. I still prayed, asking for patience, strength, and guidance. I savored many quiet moments of gratitude and tried to nap when the kids napped, but tears still came easy (theirs and mine). It was all part of this challenging season of mothering young kiddos.

Over time, my heart became a long-distance friend I'd lost touch with. But thanks to that December walk in the woods, things started to change—quickly.

Jason and I put our heads together to find creative ways to get me out on that path on a regular basis, making it a top priority. Every time I went, I found wonder. My spirit continued to receive whispers that brought new inspiration. And the lessons, wow! God was speaking, and my soul found new life. I am humbled and grateful that he got my attention.

December evenings have proven to be important on my journey, whether it's donning red tights and meeting Jason for the first time, or donning a weary heart and rediscovering wonder. Both were monumental moments of wonder and turning points in my life.

How about you? Are you feeling weary? Maybe you feel uninspired and disconnected? Is Adultitis winning most days?

Living like this can be devastating over time. It's easy to start taking yourself too seriously as you watch your passions drift away. Your heart can become heavy

and distant, and you find yourself stuck in a rut.

If you are in one of these challenging seasons, I believe you are holding this book for a reason. I'm here to walk with you on a new path of healing and growth.

What does self-care look like for you right now? Are there opportunities for improvement?

Is there someone in your life who you can ask to help support your efforts?

CHAPTER 3

Way Back When

Let's take a little trip in my time machine, back to Shady Lane. I'll park it at the end of our long driveway, which was one of my favorite places to spend countless hours. With the four K-Mart sisters, the myriad of bikes, scooters, and roller skates often prevented my dad from pulling our blue station wagon into the garage. There are no knee pads or helmets to be found here. If you look beyond the house, you'll see the swing set under the oak tree in the backyard. Now look up! There's Suzy's house. You're in the right place!

Growing up, this yard was my personal haven for wonder. Wonder was everywhere, found easily in the magical moments of discovering a fuzzy brown caterpillar in the grass and chasing the butterflies. I must've climbed that same tree in the front yard a hundred times just to see it all from a new perspective.

There I am wearing the super-short shorts with the stripes on the sides, pulling my wagon through our front ditch. Yes, my face does look a little dirty (Ha-ha, thanks for pointing that out.) My red Radio Flyer wagon is overflowing with all sorts of treasures I've collected. It appears I've made a bird nest out of sticks and mud again, and I'm about to use the leftovers to make a pretend campfire. But first, I'm stopping at the hose for a drink of water.

What I wouldn't give to spend one more day here as that younger Kim.

As the youngest of four girls, and as with most caboose children, the first decade of my life was quite different than the second. I was born into lots of activity. With three instant playmates, there were shenanigans galore, and I loved it all.

A notable truth about these years is that I prayed a lot. I suspect maybe more than the average kid, but who knows for sure?

My earliest prayers are connected to my dad. He became sick when I was young. As with most faded memories, the details are fuzzy, but I remember how I felt: sad and afraid.

I may have only been seven, but I wanted to help. I'd create handmade cards to cheer him up, using construction paper and half-dried markers. He rewarded me with generous hugs of gratitude and praise.

Mom always said prayer was the best gift. Maybe God would heal him, like a

miracle? I believed in miracles. (What kid doesn't?) At church, before bed, and during our meal-time prayers, I would ask God to heal my dad. I even tried using my birthday wishes. It was worth a try. Year after year, my prayers and wishes for his healing persisted.

Spoiler alert: Dad was never healed. He suffered from rheumatoid arthritis, which is quite a challenging diagnosis for someone to receive in his late thirties, and the sole provider for a family of six as a trained electrician. Seeing his chronic pain was painful for all of us girls.

I do remember understanding at a certain point that this illness was not curable, so I kept on praying and wishing he would receive the miracle he deserved. Anything was possible with God. All the while, I'd escape to that safe haven in my backyard wonderland for quiet and peace, which was always a gift in our busy household.

Inside, pill bottles populated the kitchen countertops and medical bills covered my mom's desk. From my swing set, I had a lot to think about and notice. I could see my mom washing dishes through the kitchen window. She spent a big portion of my childhood at that sink. (Don't all parents?) She was loyal to my dad, patiently listening to his ever-evolving list of symptoms. Little by little, she took over many of the household chores, including the yardwork, which was no small task on Shady Lane. She was gracious and compassionate, teaching me powerful lessons though her selfless example of living a life of service, the power of cheerful encouragement, and the importance of faith and prayer amidst hardships.

These lessons were taught and received every day. They rarely included words.

My childlike faith would not let me give up on praying for my dad's miracle. As I've learned after a few solid decades of prayer, it is meant to change us, not God. My need to pray and process his illness and pain was gradually changing me into a more compassionate and empathetic person. This was a miracle in and of itself, being the stereotypical self-absorbed youngest child. Looking back, it was in these faithful conversations and moments with God that he molded my heart for the work he would call me to do.

These experiences of witnessing my parents' faith provided me with countless moments of wonder and awe that I now appreciate with a little life perspective. I have strong memories of Dad praying at night before bed, his St. Joseph medal peeking out through his undershirt. He led our family with strength and grace, no matter how terrible he felt.

Mom served without complaining, praying continuously for the provisions to pay the bills on time, week after week. It was the multiplication of the loaves and fishes many times, as he'd miss out on work due to pain and surgeries. My faith

grew stronger through their collective witness. It's now a gift to acknowledge that my passion for encouraging others is tied to all of these childhood moments, many of them challenging.

What hopes and prayers did you have as a child? Why?

Thinking about your own childhood, do you suspect that certain experiences have inspired and informed your passions and purpose today?

It's not always an easy process to look back. Journeying into our childhoods can conjure up pain and loss that's tempting to leave in the shadow of yesteryear. Many people find the support of trained therapists and psychologists as helpful options on this journey of rediscovery.

However you end up making the trek in your "way back" machine, I encourage you to go slow and start with the wonder-filled moments. Lean into these positive childhood memories and see what lessons emerge. These foundational memories have the ability to heal and inform our hearts moving forward, reigniting our passions in a powerful way.

> "When you numb your pain you also numb your joy." —Brene Brown

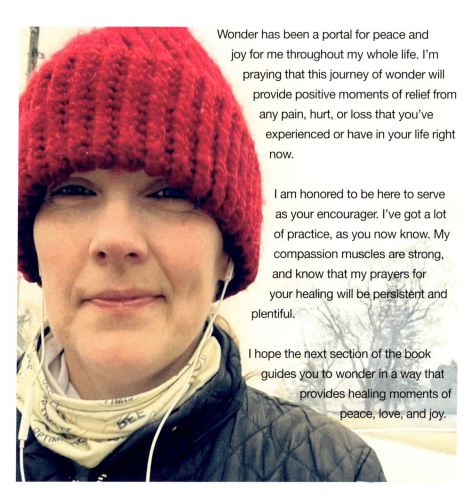

Wonder has been a portal for peace and joy for me throughout my whole life. I'm praying that this journey of wonder will provide positive moments of relief from any pain, hurt, or loss that you've experienced or have in your life right now.

I am honored to be here to serve as your encourager. I've got a lot of practice, as you now know. My compassion muscles are strong, and know that my prayers for your healing will be persistent and plentiful.

I hope the next section of the book guides you to wonder in a way that provides healing moments of peace, love, and joy.

CHAPTER 4

It's Time to Wonderhunt

This gift of wonder inspired a whole new season for me. It became a scavenger hunt for my soul. On my walks, in the peaceful, quiet moments, I found myself grabbing my phone to capture the beauty and inspiration my heart was experiencing. I am not a photographer, but I was having fun taking pictures of what I was finding.

Eventually, the pictures started to add up.

I'd share my "joyful haul" of photos with Jason and the kids, like a proud fisherman sharing pictures of my best catches from an afternoon on the lake. It was my way of revealing part of my heart with them. Every time I shared a photo that was meaningful to me, I feel like it healed my heart a little more, bringing me back into inspired and passionate living.

Like digging for treasure, this process took time, intention, persistence, and courage. Little by little, I continued to feel my heart reawakening and opening wider. It was a physical, emotional, and spiritual journey. I was seeing life through the eyes of my younger self once again, rediscovering my wild heart. It was exhilarating!

Some days I would come home and edit the photos. Other days I would write poetry to accompany the photos I had taken. This is the first time I had ever written in this style. Here's an example:

> *Oh, dear heart. Take courage and break free.*
> *The longing, whispers, visions.*
> *It's all a gift from within, asking, calling, begging for the wild—*
> *a new way of living.*
> *Wild heart, do not be afraid.*
> *Freedom is beyond what you can see.*
> *Escape.*
> *Wonder is waiting.*

[Savoring the first snow of the season, I was captured by the delight of the tiny bundles of snow that found themselves stuck in the most unexpected little places—mostly on the wildflowers. But this composition instantly struck my heart and begged me to capture it.]

I wrote dozens of these little reflections. I couldn't stop. These wonder-filled moments were inspiring me to write and reflect. The harried reality of my season of life hadn't changed, but my heart had, and this spark was fueling me daily. I had more energy, a new playfulness, and I could see that my faith was growing. I found myself shenanigating spontaneously with the kids, allowing easy wins, like dancing in the kitchen and running with the grocery cart in the parking lot. I was fun again. I was laughing louder and longer. It was an amazing transformation!

Wonder! Who knew, right?

Jason, my own personal encourager, invited me to post my pictures on Instagram, which had previously only featured shots of our cute kiddos who were growing like weeds. I hesitated. Why would anyone want to see my nature pictures? He convinced me that it would serve as a neat scrapbook of my journey. So about a year after that first December walk, I started posting my pics.

To date, I have shared well over five thousand photos.

follow kim on instagram

In our quiet moments over the years, Jason and I slowly unpacked what was unfolding for me, and we fondly started to call this journey my Wonderhunt.

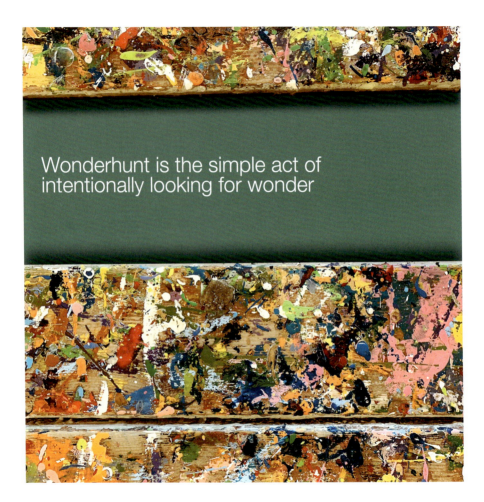

Wonderhunt is the simple act of intentionally looking for wonder

As we've discussed, the first step to finding wonder—and to Wonderhunting—is to *notice*. That's it. Lift your head. Look. See with new eyes for just a moment.

Noticing. It's a simple step, but it's not easy. The best parts of life are like that, aren't they?

Wonder can be found anywhere, but as we've processed previously, I suspect you'll most easily find it connected to positive memories from your past, or maybe even in your childhood.

The next part of this book will teach you how to Wonderhunt, inviting you to slow down and take a moment to notice the wonder that exists around you today. It's designed to be a thirty-one-day journey. Each challenge is open-ended so that you can accomplish it wherever you are and do it again and again.

Walking in the woods is not a necessary part of the process. This is your unique journey to take now. Make it your own. Be open to the wonder in your corner of the world.

Within each chapter, you will find a challenge in the form of a photo prompt meant to activate you into seeking wonder. The challenges will give you a fresh perspective on your day. Keep your eyes open, then grab a photo to capture the moment as it arises.

After you reflect on what you experienced, reopen this book and use the QR code in each chapter to access our online community of fellow Wonderhunters. In order to gain access, you'll need to create an account in our private online community, the Escape Adulthood League. Do this by visiting **www.EscapeAdulthood.me**. Once you're logged in, the QR codes will take you to each of the 31 challenges. If you download the Mighty Network app, you can also access these same links in the EA League by visiting *Escape Labs*, then *Wonderhunt*.

Let's talk about the photos for a moment. Although I've included a fun photo tip for each challenge, please remember that this process is less about mastering photography and more about seeing with new eyes. The tips are here to enhance your experience and invite you to try new techniques. Let me emphasize one thing: there's no need for a fancy camera; a smartphone will work great (that's what I use). If you can push the button to take a picture, you're prepared. And if you happen to be a seasoned photographer, the prompts may inspire you get your creative juices flowing in new ways.

Enjoy the inspiration included throughout from our fellow Wonderhunters. Their stories and photos are a gift to each of us on this journey.

I think you're ready to start noticing wonder. Together, I believe we will find it.

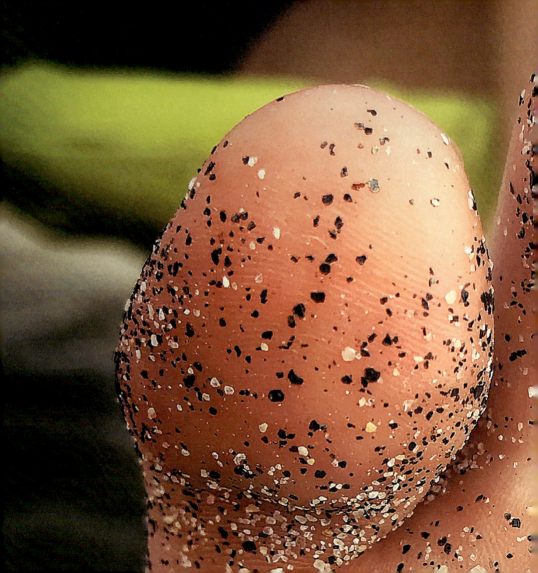

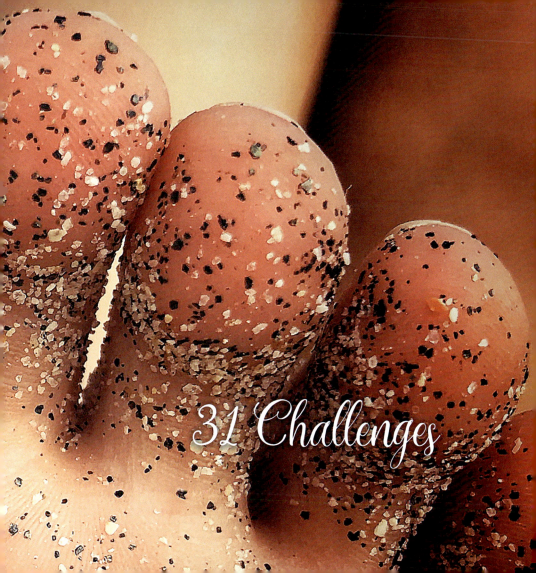

WHOLEHEARTED LIVING

Highlight something that is both broken and beautiful.

Our hearts are wounded, filled with bumps, scrapes, holes. It's impossible to identify all of the hardships that have led us to our present state of being, from epic battles to the most microscopic hurts. And yet, our hearts are beautiful.

The discovery of this leaf took my breath away. It showed such fragility and strength. Even amidst the brokenness, it still maintained its shape. Our hearts are similar: capable of hurt and happiness—and unique beauty. Open your eyes to the beauty of the brokenness.

> *"If you can't get a miracle, become one."*
> *–Nick Vujicic*

share your find

#wonderhunt

fellow wonderhunter

"These are my mother's hands. They are so broken and twisted by arthritis that she struggles to get them to do what she wants. But they have done so much and taught me so many things over the years that they are still beautiful to me!" –Catherine Schofield

photo tip

Our eyes are drawn to symmetry. In photography, both symmetry and asymmetry bring about countless opportunities for creativity. Asymmetrical photos demonstrate unequal visual weight from one side to another. Tinker with this by placing the object you're shooting off-center, or find an object that doesn't have symmetry, then let the imperfection shine.

wonder workout!

Spend some time today seeking healing. Allow your heart the space to feel the brokenness. Then, seek peace within the hurt in order to bring a new perspective and open the floodgates of growth.

i wonder...

What challenges in your present situation will add to your life's story in a beautiful way, bringing potential for growth and opportunity?

SUNNY SIDE UP

Capture an image that allows the sun to be the centerpiece.

The glaring sun through the canopy of trees revealed such a stark contrast between darkness and light. It got me thinking about how often the sun plays a powerful role in healing my heart. I find myself standing in the light, stopping all movement, inviting the rays to reach me. The more I savor the sun, the more it guides me to clearer thinking.

Lean into the sun and allow the beauty of the light to call you. Step courageously out of the darkness, trusting that joy, peace, and a path meant just for you lies beyond the darkness.

"Travel light. Live light. Spread the light. Be the light."
–Yogi Bhajan

share your find

#wonderhunt

fellow wonderhunter

"After a nine-mile hike, this liquid sunshine was exactly what I needed. Then the sun itself peeked out from behind a cloud and made it that much more glorious!" –Nic Russo

photo tip
The sun can mess up a photo, but it's also fun to play with. I love trying to capture sun flares. A simple way to do this is to use an object in the shot to partially hide the sun (a building, yard ornament, or a tree). Not only will you catch a neat flare, but it will also add a magical, artistic aspect to the object that's highlighted. Play with the angles as you move around until you capture the photo that speaks directly to you.

wonder workout!
Write a list of things that inspire you. Pick one from the list and find a way to incorporate it into your day today as a way to reignite your heart, inviting the light back in.

i wonder...
What is your relationship with the sun? How does it interconnect on your journey with the light and darkness of life?

A BIT OF SILLINESS

Photograph something that is undeniably silly.

Driving by this fabulous, whimsical find, of course we had to turn around. I needed this picture! Silliness is something I'm pretty serious about. It's powerful, after all, being the gateway to good living. Although not always easy to attain in the day-to-day, it must be sought after with great intention.

Don't underestimate the effort it takes to be silly, especially in times of extreme stress and anxiety. But it is possible. Some days it requires a U-turn. Make the effort to seek that which is silly. This will lead to healing, hope, and happiness. It is truly good for your heart!

"There's power in looking silly and not caring that you do."
–Amy Poehler

share your find

#wonderhunt

fellow wonderhunter

"What are you looking at? I love googly eyes and have been placing them strategically around the house. It helps me keep an eye on my quarantine partners so they don't eat all the Easter candy. The eyeball on this duck artwork almost looks like it belongs though. Thinking about silliness this morning opened up my whole day to a slew of silly ideas." –Katja Schindler

photo tip
Our eyes love variety, which means contrast can be quite a playground in photography. It could be contrasting colors, tones, sizes, textures, shapes, or saturation. Look for an extreme contrast of some sort and celebrate their differences.

wonder workout!
If you've never seen the movie *Finding Neverland* with Johnny Depp, Kate Winslet, and Dustin Hoffman, then check it out. I guarantee it will inspire you to increase the number of silly moments you allow yourself to experience each day.

i wonder...
When was the last time you were silly in front someone else? I mean super silly! Has it been too long? If so, why?

COURAGEOUS COLOR

Take a photo featuring color in a way that fills your heart with joy.

I love visiting Mexico. Culturally, their passion for color makes my heart sing. We all need a splash of lime green every once in a while. As adults, we like safe, predictable outcomes. Adultitis loves to keep us playing life small, serious, and colored with shades of taupe. Snore.

What are you waiting for? It's time to be a bit radical. Dig deeper for the courage to face fear and doubt and take that next step anyway. This brave act will renew your childlike spirit in a way that will change everything!

"When we're not afraid anymore, we can start doing stuff."
—Bob Goff

share your find

#wonderhunt

fellow wonderhunter

"At work, we have a path that I walk every day during lunch. Excited to jump into the Wonderhunt today, I got to work a little early so that I could start. Here's what's amazing: I actually took a few photos of different colors that I had never noticed before. I walk this path every day, and the colors had become like white noise to me. I walked around giddy like a school boy, discovering new colors."
–Michael Leone

photo tip
Remember "follow the leader" as a kid? You can do this with your pictures by playing with the composition to highlight a diagonal line across the frame. Take the viewer on a journey with their eyes to highlight a focal point. This intentional artistic flow will bring your photos interesting depth and perspective.

wonder workout!
Write down the fears and doubts that are limiting you and preventing you from living with a brave, bold, and beautiful spirit. Bringing them to the light will diminish their power and help to renew a spirit of radical courage within you.

i wonder...
What do you need bold courage to do right now? What's the next obvious step?

SURPRISE YOURSELF

Take a selfie unlike any other you've taken, revealing an emotion that is not often captured.

Cautious. Wandering. Inspired. Distant. This is how I'd describe myself here. It was a calm and reflective moment that I'm glad was recorded. I'm hard-pressed to find a selfie that doesn't reflect the three most popular selfie emotions: happiness, excitement, and silliness. And yet, what percentage of the day represents these emotions? We embody a wide range of feelings each day, sometimes hundreds before lunch. Embrace them. This helps us to love and appreciate who we are. Own the variety as a gift to yourself—one of self-awareness, acceptance, and compassion.

> *"God has given you grace. Maybe you should give yourself some too."*
> Todd Stocker

share your find

#wonderhunt

fellow wonderhunter

"I'm often this goofy at home and with my close friends, but rarely this way in public anymore. Had to try out one of the mustaches I bought to hand out at the end of the month. Quality control. #mustacheforthewin!" –Mary Eickemeyer

photo tip
Draw an imaginary tic-tac-toe grid on the frame of your picture (better yet, add grid lines in your camera settings). Play with the Rule of Thirds as a composition guideline by putting your subject (in this case, yourself) in the right or left third of the frame. Our eyes love it when the subject is off-center because it looks more natural, bringing welcome balance.

wonder workout!
Identify at least five describing words that come to mind when you look at your selfie, words that express who you are right now and how you feel in this unique moment in time.

i wonder...
What surprised you about the selfie you captured? What does this say about your current emotional state?

REROUTE WITH GRACE

Capture something that represents resilience.

The persistence of this dandelion blew my mind! I struggled to comprehend its tenacity and grace. It represents the strength and hope of what is possible after pain and brokenness. There's something sacred about this invitation to be resilient.

Dig deep, accessing strength from your roots in order to experience the true power of grit, creativity, and determination, embracing this twisting and turning detour into the unknown. You can choose to remain broken or find a new route back toward the light. Borrow courage from this delightful weed (soon to be wish) and rise.

> *"The oak fought the wind and was broken, the willow bent when it must and survived."*
> –Robert Jordan

share your find

#wonderhunt

fellow wonderhunter • • • • • • • • • • • •

"This flower hung on when all the others let go at the end of the season. Sometimes I hang on until I am ready to try something new… but it is good to know others are there, have been where I have been and can offer support." –Jen DeRidder

photo tip

Look for "vignette" in your editing tools. A vignette is a darker border around the edges of the picture compared to the center, sometimes presenting as a shadow or blur. This is an effect you can use in editing to help lesson distracting elements in the photo, and it helps to draw attention to a particular part of the image.

wonder workout!

Identify what is preventing you from being more resilient right now? Talk this out with a trusted friend, one who generously extends grace and love.

i wonder...

Is the opportunity to be resilient presenting itself? Are you leaning into it or resisting the next step?

SEEING SEPIA

Photograph something you savor.

I loved these sunglasses. The lenses shifted everything to a neat sepia tone, enhancing the colors around me, making for a romantic view of life. I never wanted to take them off. We all have experiences in life when we feel like living is easy, for once. The glass isn't just half full, it's overflowing! When they cracked, I was left with this question: How do we appreciate the good things in life? First, we can start by paying attention. Identify the moment as a gift, and savor it in your heart, even just for a moment. It's as simple and as hard as that. Next, we can seek opportunities that we know will be rewarding in our hearts. This requires us to make time and space for receiving beautiful moments.

> *"I've always believed in savoring the moments. In the end, they are the only things we'll have."*
> —Anna Godbersen

share your find

#wonderhunt

fellow wonderhunter

"When our neighbor is finished harvesting almonds this time of year, he lets me go through his orchard and pick any that remain. I savor spending hours walking through these groves and getting almonds. Sometimes the orchard is full of the music of birds chirping. Other times it's powerfully silent. We could transform our lives if we filled our days with hours we savor." –Sharon Niman Lundgren

photo tip

The direction of the light has the potential to make your picture more intriguing. The angle from which the light hits your subject will shape the viewers' perception of the appearance. Light entering from the side will highlight texture and form while also creating shadows. Front light shows details but can leave out the texture. Move around your object and play with the light.

wonder workout!

Make a list of things you want to savor more. Keep the list somewhere you will see it to help you remember your desire to appreciate the moments you treasure.

i wonder...

What is something that is easy for you to savor? What prevents you from savoring life more fully in your day-to-day life?

RECLAIM JOY

Find something that brings you joy.

Our son's nickname is Sunshine Boy. He has the ability to light up a room in 1.7 seconds. His spirit is unleashed. I long to find this level of joy again. In the moments when I do, I feel free to be uniquely me, dreaming big and opening my heart to risk and love without holding anything back. It's amazing!

Fighting Adultitis amidst the exhaustion and the overwhelm of this journey is a haul. It requires you to dig deep. Reclaim this joyful spirit by choosing to do so.

"Joy, collected over time, fuels resilience."
–Brené Brown

share your find

#wonderhunt

fellow wonderhunter

"This snapshot is emblematic of deep joy to me on many levels – place, people, passion, and presence. Whether Lake Mendota or Lake Powell – places of affecting natural beauty, shades of color, water, warmth, and sunlight. I am with people – a band of brothers I have known for at least twenty years. I am experiencing the fun and thrill of water skiing – a passion that is life-giving to my soul. I am in a time and place where I experience the presence of God – who is altogether love and grace, speaking and silent, powerful and personal, and filled with wonder and joy." –Rich Henderson

photo tip

Joy is often found in action, which means there's potential for blurriness. Our phones have an awesome feature called Burst Mode/Shot, allowing rapid-fire captures, sometimes up to one hundred shots. Since every device is a little different, if you're not sure how this works, a quick Internet search will help. The fun part is reviewing all of the shots and identifying that perfectly joyful moment.

wonder workout!

Share a joyful story from your childhood with someone you love, and invite them to share a joyful memory from their younger years.

i wonder...

What memory from your childhood brings you joy? Revisit this memory for a few moments today.

NOTHING TO SEE HERE

Use your camera to reveal something that is hidden.

Remember invisible markers? First, you write a message with the white marker, then you color over it to reveal what was once invisible. Pure magic! They remind me of the day I ended up in the prairie before sunrise on a chilly morning. The combination of the temperature, the angle of the sun, and the mist revealed a hidden surprise: spider webs galore. What a gift to see their artistry.

See with new eyes today—the eyes of your camera lens. There is wonder and magic waiting for you.

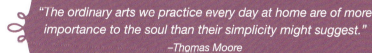

"The ordinary arts we practice every day at home are of more importance to the soul than their simplicity might suggest."
–Thomas Moore

share your find

#wonderhunt

fellow wonderhunter

"Walking into the house after a heavy snow one day, I noticed my little garden angel was being embraced by its own guardian angel. Guess we can all use a hug and a little help now and again, right?"
–Ronda Ramsdell

photo tip

I love close-ups, especially for objects in nature. When capturing the details of an object, forget your zoom; instead, move as close as you can and keep your hand extra steady to maximize the quality of resolution. Tap the screen to focus the image, and be patient, giving your camera a few seconds. If your image looks fuzzy, move back and experiment with the depth to find the right distance to clearly capture the details.

wonder workout!

Dig deep for the courage required to share your hidden gift, skill, or passion with someone you trust. Pick a person who will encourage you on your journey, and ask for their accountability and support.

i wonder...

Do you have a gift, skill, or passion that has become hidden that you would like to rediscover? How can you reveal its true beauty again?

FACING THE DAY

Highlight something from a new angle.

The book *Miracle Mornings* by Hal Elrod was a game-changer for me. It's about transforming your life before 8:00 a.m. Instead of starting my day reacting to my emotions, I now begin with intention and peace. My formula is simple: a candle, journal, Bible, book of choice, earbuds for music, and coffee. Sixty minutes later and my heart and head are prepared to embrace the day with faith, optimism, and joy.

You have the power to shift the opportunities of the day ahead by approaching it from a new perspective.

"The morning is the size of heaven. What will you do with it?"
–Mark Doty

share your find

#wonderhunt

fellow wonderhunter

"This is the back side of a dead-end sign. I think we often forget that when we hit a dead end, we can simply turn around to face a world of bountiful solutions and opportunities." –Michelle McNulty

photo tip
Some of the most creative photos have to do with a change in perspective. Your chosen viewpoint has a significant impact. hen you shift what angle the camera is coming from, it highlights something specific because of that choice, drastically impacting the relationship between the objects in unique ways.

wonder workout!
Identify a rut you're in that frustrates and limits your ability to be open to new possibilities. Do one thing today to shift the direction, allowing for a new action or way of thinking in this area of your life.

i wonder...
Are you in a rut with your morning routine? How can you make it more intentional and life-giving?

WHERE'S WHIMSY?

Find whimsy.

One of my favorite portals for finding wonder is through whimsy. This goat embodies it. After looking at photos from the zoo, our daughter stopped at this goat and said, "This picture frames your life, Mom." When asked why, she shared three words: curious, weird, confused. I took this as the compliment she meant it to be.

She's onto something. Embrace curiosity and allow yourself to be weird. Be brave enough to remain a little confused on the journey, and childlike wonder and whimsy are sure to follow.

> *"Too much whimsy and no one takes you seriously. Just the right amount and the world takes notice."*
> *–Jason Kotecki*

share your find

#wonderhunt

fellow wonderhunter

"The Loyalty Building was where our company was headquartered until 1914, but it reminds me of the moving staircases from the Harry Potter movies. Curiosity led us up many flights and down mysterious hallways. Secrets and places unknown beckoned us, and the fact that we pretty much had the place to ourselves made it feel like we were first years and breaking all the rules." –Mike Schroeder

photo tip
When you spot something you'd like to photograph, see if there's an opportunity to creatively frame the subject. Step back and look for a natural frame using elements from the foreground or background (clouds, branches, shadows, doorways). This composition technique helps guide where the viewers' eyes will focus within the shot.

wonder workout!
Look at what you're wearing today. Find a way to add a little whimsy to the mix—just a little. See if it adds any fun to your day.

i wonder...
Whimsy is my thing! What is your thing? What lights you up, and how often is this a part of your life?

SEE WITH NEW EYES

Reveal a silhouette that resembles an inkblot test.

Pretty cool T-Rex tree, right? That's what my imagination saw, anyway. Remember the inkblot tests from psychology class called the Rorschach Test? Perceptions of inkblots are recorded and analyzed using interpretation and algorithms. What we visually perceive is based on our individual makeup. What you see may never be seen by anyone else, ever. Wow, right?

Take a needed escape and welcome the fantastical and curious child that exists within. Have fun asking the question, "What might this be?"

> *"And no one puts new wine into old wineskins; otherwise the wine will burst the skins, and the wine is lost and the skins as well; but one puts new wine into fresh wineskins."* –Mark 2:22

share your find

#wonderhunt

fellow wonderhunter

"I spent so much time yesterday looking for silhouettes. Then, this morning, inspiration came. Sometimes you have to look, and look again, in order to see something completely different." –Alison West

photo tip

Capture a stunning silhouette by shooting the camera toward the sun, positioning your subject with the light source hiding behind it. Pick something with distinct lines that is interesting to the eye. Try to find a simple, uncluttered background that allows your subject to stand out and shine vibrantly. If you shoot from a lower angle, you allow yourself more sky, making the silhouette even more distinct.

wonder workout!

Share your photo with a friend, family member, or coworker, then ask the classic question, "What might this be?" See if it's anything close to what you perceived when you first took the photo.

i wonder...

When's the last time you imagined the best-case scenario when faced with a challenge, using your creativity for good, versus fearing the worst?

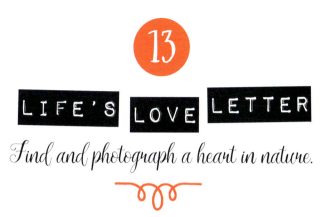

LIFE'S LOVE LETTER

Find and photograph a heart in nature.

A few years ago, hearts started showing up in my life just when I needed them. The more I looked, the more I found. My own heart opened wider with each treasure found. I felt loved. I felt I was not alone as my heart was transforming on my Wonderhunt journey. Keep your eyes (and your heart) open to finding a heart and see what happens. What you place your focus on expands. Hearts represent love, forgiveness, healing, and peace. Finding unexpected representations of them is God's way of using an earthly symbol to send a message of love and a promise of guidance from him. Be open to receiving a message from nature and the love that exists for you. Everything is interconnected.

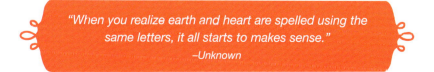

"When you realize earth and heart are spelled using the same letters, it all starts to makes sense."
–Unknown

share your find

#wonderhunt

fellow wonderhunter

"I often think and pray for others (my wife and kids in particular) that they will feel, in a tangible way, how much they are loved by God. But rarely do I ask the same for myself. I hope that this experience will help me remember how loved I am. It's in this love I know I will find the deepest kind of peace and joy." –Drew Pistilli

photo tip
A photo is made up of positive and negative shapes. Positive shapes are the objects in the frame, while the negative shapes are the areas between the objects. Keep an eye out for the shapes found in the negative space. This space shares the edges with the object, creating an outline. Keeping an open and curious mind will help you to identify what you might have initially missed.

wonder workout!
Draw a heart shape on a piece of paper. Write a message inside, something you hear your heart saying to you on this journey. Put this picture someplace special so that you'll see it frequently.

i wonder...
Were you able to find a heart? What is your heart telling you from this experience of seeking a heart in nature?

THRILL OF THE CHASE

Chase something and take a picture of the pursuit.

Hide-and-seek was always my favorite game as a child. Stomping around in the snow to find the light, I was astounded at what I discovered in my wanderings. I found myself staring straight down this magically lit path at my very own heart center. It took my breath away.

What we're seeking has been inside of us all along and is actually seeking us. Most days we are the ones hiding. Open yourself up to the chase. Invite healing, inspiration, and a hope that goes beyond understanding to find a new way inside your heart.

> *"What lies behind us and what lies ahead of us are tiny matters compared to what lies within us."*
> –Henry David Thoreau

share your find

#wonderhunt

fellow wonderhunter

"I noticed this stream that runs through my town. I go by it and glance at it every day. I cross the bridges to go various places. No matter how slow my day might be or how many things have been slowed down or cancelled, the one thing I can always count on is the movement of the stream. It always runs no matter what."
–Fr. Dave Timmerman

photo tip
Draw the viewer's eye toward a specific focal point using leading lines. These are natural lines that you can use to position and frame (roads, doorways, railroad tracks, shorelines). It's a simple way to add structure and drama. If the lines aren't obvious, put yourself in an odd position—try standing on a chair, laying upside down, or peeking around a corner.

wonder workout!
Make a list of things you desire, such as your dreams and hopes for the future. Circle the one that jumps off the page, then promise yourself that you'll seek this desire with an open heart.

i wonder...
What are you seeking deep within your heart? What are you doing to pursue this chase?

MIRROR MIRROR

Photograph something that represents your current state of emotions.

I love noticing flowers in their various stages of blooming and withering. This one stopped me in my tracks. Everyone loves a sunflower; it's always so optimistic and happy. But this closed blossom—folded up and pulled in—is a relatable image. I love the beautiful honesty displayed here. It's a gift to see ourselves in the wild. It's validating, freeing.

Open your eyes in a new way to discover something that connects to your own heart, bringing a new level of self-awareness and insight to where you are and where you are heading.

"Beauty begins the moment you decide to be yourself."
–Coco Chanel

share your find

#wonderhunt

fellow wonderhunter

"I was totally at peace when I took this, and there was no Internet to post it (which is probably why I was totally at peace)." –Nick Adkins

photo tip
Allow your picture to evoke an emotional reaction by using the element of surprise. It could be an image that speaks for itself based on the circumstances, or you can nudge the emotions along using tools within your control, such as the weather (fog vs. sunshine), lighting, time of day, color contrasts, framing, etc. Tinker with the tools you've learned in the previous challenges to capture a surprise.

wonder workout!
Spend a few minutes looking at yourself in the mirror. Take a fresh look. Focus on your eyes first, then examine the rest of your face and your unique features. Invite your heart to extend love generously, even if you find yourself noticing flaws before beauty. Embrace peace with the person you see in the reflection.

i wonder...
What part of nature are you drawn to right now? What is the message for you?

WILD CHILD

Reveal something that is wild and free.

Our youngest is the wild child of our family (many are). One Sunday at church, I heard her singing loudly and confidently, without knowing any of the words. Was this a case of radical courage or pure innocence? Probably both. As adults, our own wild hearts become bruised and weary. It's challenging to reignite the passion we once had so naturally as kids, but we can try.

Look for the "wild and free" out there! Being more lighthearted will bring you one step closer to reopening that courageous and innocent part of your heart, inspiring a new—and maybe even wild—song once again.

> *"And now," cried Max, "let the wild rumpus start."*
> –Maurice Sendak, excerpt from *Where the Wild Things Are*

share your find

#wonderhunt

fellow wonderhunter

"I love fields of wildflowers! The flowers grow through all of the weeds and (perceived) chaos around them, reaching up to bring glory to the Creator in their beauty. I want to be like a wildflower. Amidst all the chaos around me, I aim to be a light of beauty that points to heaven."
–Judee Howard

photo tip
Arrange your composition to have an odd number of objects. If you have an even number, just zoom in or out of the frame in order to naturally compose the shot to highlight an odd quantity. Designers, speakers, and writers (see what I did there?) constantly use this rule in their work because odd numbers are more interesting and pleasing to the eyes and ears.

wonder workout!
Make a point today to do something you would label as "wild and free."

i wonder...
What techniques (heart hacks) have you found effective in helping to reawaken your wild side? How often do you implement these strategies intentionally?

17
THE MAKING OF A MOMENT

Make a special moment with someone and reveal the beauty found there.

While doing dishes, I looked out the window and noticed it was golden hour and knew the sky was foreshadowing something amazing. Also known as "magic hour," this special time arrives just before sunset (and just after sunrise), where the lighting is soft and warm, with golden and reddish-pink tones. I grabbed the kids and off we went, having no idea that this would be one of the most beautiful sunsets we'd ever see. It's a memory I'll savor forever. Intentionality and spontaneity are a powerful mix. When these elements are brought together, you can transform a seemingly inconsequential moment into something impactful. Do this on a regular basis, and you'll have created a lifetime of meaningful moments and memories to treasure.

> *"It isn't the great big pleasures that count the most, it's making a great deal out of the little ones."*
> –Jean Webster

share your find

#wonderhunt

fellow wonderhunter

This captures a moment when the one-and-only love of my life stepped into my shot of the city I have loved since the moment I arrived. He is walking our dog, Taika. The moment we laid eyes on her we knew she would give us endless amounts of unconditional love. This photo captures all my favorite moments! This is love! This is a reminder to appreciate all that is in front of us!" –Theresa Hamari

photo tip
Our eyes naturally find the horizon, that line that separates the land from the sky. Horizontal lines in photography have a way of bringing a sense of stability and peace to a shot. Sometimes this can feel a bit too static or dull. If you're able to break the horizon with a perpendicular vertical line, this adds helpful tension and variety for the viewer.

wonder workout!
Identify a list of the people you would like to share a special moment with. Arrange for the opportunity to spend time with them (even if only by phone or virtually) in the next few weeks.

i wonder...
When's the last time intention and spontaneity brought you a meaningful moment with someone you love?

18

WINNING AT TWINNING

Uncover an act of twinning.

I would never have guessed that our daughter would've found herself twinning in this fabulous shirt. Life is awesome like that some days. I find that when I get stressed, I exist in survival mode. I hide, becoming camouflaged and stuck in a zone that cuts me off from inspiration, passion, and a purposeful life. This is a scary place because it can last a long time if I'm not paying attention.

Look honestly at yourself today. Commit to the hunt of rediscovering a more vibrant state of living, one that helps you stand apart.

> *"Why fit in when you were born to stand out?"*
> *–Dr. Seuss*

share your find

#wonderhunt

fellow wonderhunter

"Is it a mirror reflection? Kinda. We complement each other, having traveled this path together since 1982. We are alike in many fundamental ways, and have been comfortable with each other from the very beginning. Yet we are also 'opposite sides of the mirror' too. I'm loud, happy in crowds, and silly. She's quiet, likes her solitude, and has a more serious disposition. Yet we are reflections of a single heart." –Jim Kramer

photo tip
Embrace one single vibrant color as an effective tool to let simplicity shine in your photograph. Find subjects that do not contain a lot of detail—the less visual clutter the better when highlighting bright colors. It's fun to enhance the colors even more by tinkering with the contrast, saturation, and white balance settings in your editing tools.

wonder workout!
One way to jump out of the shadows is to embrace your weird side. We tend to think that 93 percent is an optimal amount to share with the world. Do something weird in an effort to break free from a camouflaged state of being.

i wonder...
Is there a part of yourself that has been hidden that you'd like to bring back to the surface?

LOOKING UP

Look up and discover something that was there all along.

During a trip to the island of Oahu in Hawaii, I couldn't stop staring at the fabulous trees. They are so different than here in the Midwest. This magical canopy reminded me that there is a lot to see when I keep my head up. Instead of getting distracted in the overwhelm of the details of life, looking up helps me remain open to the whispers that provide wonder, possibility, and hope. Inevitably, new opportunities follow when we keep our perspective fresh.

Take a look at what you might be missing. There are gifts within reach when you stop to see them.

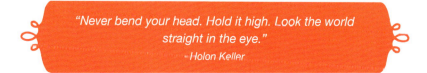

"Never bend your head. Hold it high. Look the world straight in the eye."
-Helen Keller

share your find

#wonderhunt

fellow wonderhunter

"I've been spending more time in our backyard, in the garden, and on the patio lately, which I absolutely love. Tonight I paused to take in the twinkly lights above that give the space a warm glow at night."
–Kristin Zurovitch

photo tip
As if you're looking in a magnifying glass, fill the entire frame with the image you're capturing. Move closer to the object, or use your zoom lens to eliminate all of the dead space around the edges. Celebrate the textures and patterns found with this composition technique. Don't worry about a single focal point; the equal emphasis creates visual harmony.

wonder workout!
Write down one possible opportunity for refocus in your life, a shift to move away from one thing to something better. Put a sticky note on your fridge with a word that reminds you of this refocus.

i wonder...
Are you focusing on the wrong things? What prevents you from seeing what's most important?

PROOF OF LIFE

Show evidence of the fun you had today.

I despise wet socks! Luckily, these whimsical boots have allowed for many dry walks though the prairie over the years. Sometimes the answer to life's annoyances can be the simple act of adding a little fun. Yes, the black boots were available, but these made my heart sing, which is always a sign of doing life right.

We take ourselves far too seriously, and yet our souls need fun. Pleasure and enjoyment are underappreciated by most grown-ups. Intervene in your own life! Bring balance to the chaos around you. Utilize the simple act of fun as the next step toward a lifetime of awesome.

"There's no fear when you're having fun."
—Will Thomas

share your find

#wonderhunt

fellow wonderhunter

"'A good time was had by all' is a great way to summarize yesterday and this journey of Wonderhunting. Since starting, while also adjusting to stay-at-home life, I do feel like it's gotten easier (most days) to find the simple joys of life. Yesterday, my wife and I watched a concert online, then in the evening we played a virtual game called Thirty-One with her family. It's not the crazy, jam-packed kind of Memorial Day weekend we're used to, but it was just as good—if not better." –Jeff Zagoudis

photo tip
Our eyes love complementary colors, the colors that are opposite each other on the color wheel. They naturally create the strongest contrast, which is why our eyes are drawn to them. Three pairs are: red and green, yellow and purple, and orange and blue. Tinker with the contrasts of color in the frame to see how it pops.

wonder workout!
Write down the elements of your perfect day. Specifically notice where fun is woven into it all. Find a creative way to intentionally bring that same kind of fun into your day today, even though the framework of the day may be different.

i wonder...
What's one way you can add some fun to your daily routine?

BLESSED ARE THE CREATIVE

Photograph something that could be reimagined as something else.

It was a crisp morning when I saw this hot-air balloon lifting off into the prairie. It required a double-take. Turns out, it was just my imagination taking flight. But once I saw my perspective, I couldn't unsee it. Creativity is endangered. We need to feed it daily to ensure its place in our future. As children, we were all creative. Would you call yourself creative today? Checkbox education and our constantly interrupted lifestyles have stifled our imaginations and snuffed out our ability to see through a creative lens. Gift yourself the space and time to let your mind (and heart) wander and wonder in order to discover something new.

> *"Imagination is more important than knowledge."*
> –Albert Einstein

share your find

#wonderhunt

fellow wonderhunter

"I do think being creative is a strength of mine. My favorite thing to do on a hike is to let my imagination run a little wild and create stories. A way to practice this is to try to see what a creature or child might see in my surroundings. When I noticed this decaying tree stump, I couldn't help seeing a skyline. Maybe it was a city for bugs, or a literal birds-eye view of one for a soaring chickadee!" –Rachel Crimmins

photo tip
Organize the composition of your subject from left to right, allowing a flow that is natural to our Western world (reading left to right). Our eyes love this predictable flow because it's neurologically natural. Invite the viewer to follow the visual directional forces in the shot that invite movement, creating good energy.

wonder workout!
Think about a creative endeavor that you were a part of as a child. What about this project brought you joy? Is there any part of it you can recreate today?

i wonder...
How would your life change if you invited creativity over to play, like an old friend?

GOING UNDERCOVER

Photograph something from underneath.

Remember the Smurfs, the fictional colony of tiny blue forest creatures who lived in mushroom-shaped houses? Seeing life through their eyes was mysterious and magical. One of my favorite ways to capture nature is from underneath. It often requires a spontaneous technique of shooting the image without actually seeing what you're photographing. Ten out of ten shots are terrible, but that eleventh one is often amazing.

Savor the surprises you reveal from this undercover, wait-and-see approach. It's proof that sometimes being haphazard can produce some happy accidents.

> *"Expect the unexpected. Life is full of wonderful things just waiting to surprise you."*
> –Unknown

share your find

#wonderhunt

fellow wonderhunter

"When I placed my phone to shoot straight up, magical things happened I needed to see, revealing the heart in the gnarled section of bark on the left. I failed out of college after the first few years. I took classes and stayed connected to campus in the following years. Talk about a gnarled section of life! I struggled with why I had failed and wrestled with where I belonged. In those difficult years of uncertainty, I met people who would make a huge impact on my life. If I had graduated on time, we might not have met, let alone become lifelong friends. Mine was not a straight path, but it was where my heart needed to be." –Jenna Regis

photo tip

Your camera is tiny, but you are not, which is why it's fun to let it capture perspectives and shots you would never be able to see with your own two eyes. Think low/high angles and small nooks and crannies. Don't be afraid to stick your phone somewhere silly (just hold on tight) and take lots of shots to see what you get. Check your photos and go back for more, adjusting your angle, lighting, and focus as necessary.

wonder workout!

It's nice to take a break from intentionality once in a while. One day soon, wake up and give yourself permission to play hooky. Let the day turn into a wonder-filled adventure led by your hidden desires for fun and rest.

i wonder...

What is a happy accident that has occurred in your life that has brought great blessings?

HONEY I SHRUNK MYSELF

Magnify something by flipping your camera upside down.

When I was little, I wanted to grow up—quick. Late bedtimes, freedom from school, and endless desserts sounded amazing. It didn't help being the youngest (aka "last to do everything!"). It's a universal travesty that kids want to grow up fast while grown-ups would give anything to be a kid again. Instead of getting stuck in the woes of aging, intentionally place the horizon above you in order to gain a new perspective. Revisit your childlike wonder and awe, and renew a playfulness and spontaneity that brings refreshing gifts of hope, inspiration, and possibility to your grown-up self.

> *"No, we don't need more sleep. It's our souls that are tired, not our bodies. We need nature. We need magic. We need adventure. We need freedom. We need truth. We need stillness. We don't need more sleep, we need to wake up and live."* –Brooke Hampton

share your find

#wonderhunt

fellow wonderhunter

"When I became a mom, I started to lose my imagination. I was stuck in a place of worry, anxiousness, and Adultitis. I could no longer see the fun, the beauty around me, or even shapes in the clouds above. I turned my phone upside down to catch this dandelion in a different way. It reminded me of the movie *A Bug's Life*. I imagined, 'What if I was a little bug and could grab on to that dandelion stem and float through the sky to view the world from above?' The negative thoughts and worries whisked away, making me so happy! I realized that just because I am older doesn't mean I can't enjoy those fairy tale moments. I need them more than ever." –Kelsey Schneider

photo tip

One simple technique to capturing dramatic photos is to flip your phone upside down, giving the shot a unique perspective. If you're focused on one specific object, then this straight-on angle will serve like a magnifying glass. Be sure to hold your camera still! Better yet, balance it on something solid. Increase the light in the shot, then tap the image of the object on the screen to gain clarity of focus.

wonder workout!

Remember back to your reasons for wanting to grow up when you were little. Do one of them this week.

i wonder...

What advice would your seven-year-old self have for you today?

EGGSCELLENT

Find something that has taken on a new shape.

Broken yolks happen. But this was a first! It reminds me that every time the heart breaks, it opens just a little wider to new possibilities. This invites new levels of compassion, empathy, and understanding for others who find themselves faced with similar hurts.

Although it's not easy to keep on the sunny side amidst the seasons of brokenness, eventually time and healing gift you with new clarity for your passions and purpose, leaving you to wonder if this depth of beauty could've happened any other way. Sometimes it's what we survive that gives us our shine.

> *"Joy is a decision, a really brave one, about how you are going to respond to life."*
> –Wess Stafford

share your find

#wonderhunt

fellow wonderhunter

"This gorgeous vine started out as a sweet potato! Instead of making its way into a delicious Thanksgiving dish smothered with marshmallows, this spud was forgotten—spending what might have been its last days in a cabinet alongside a few onions. Once discovered, we placed it in a jar of water. It did so well, we were able to plant a few of the slips into two flower pots! What once seemed 'broken' made way for something beautiful. It's fun to see new leaves sprout (which look like hearts!) and watch this guy grab onto nearby plants, pieces of art, and anything else nearby!" –Cara Tracy

photo tip
Keep an eye out for a unique shape that you can highlight, adding an interesting element to your photo. The lines can help lead the eye of the viewer. Our eyes are attracted to circles that hold our attention over time. Triangles are stable and can bring balance to a composition, and S-curves generate energy and flow. Using a bold, eye-catching subject matter is one way to start.

wonder workout!
If you could pick one thing to look different in your life in the next year, what would it be? Add a picture that represents this change, and place it on your bathroom mirror.

i wonder...
Have you survived something that now empowers your passions and purpose?

WINDOW WONDER

Reveal something wonder-filled from the inside looking out.

Anne Frank is known for being hidden away inside as a young teenager for two years during the Nazi occupation. Her famous diary serves as a glimpse inside the horrific reality that many suffered and was a tool for survival during this long period of her short life.

When we get stuck inside for long periods, cooped up due to sickness, quarantining, or bad weather, often a window serves as our only view out into the world. Try to use the pane of glass as a portal to new possibilities and perspectives. Intentionally observe with new eyes until you land on a unique discovery.

"The greatest day in the history of the world is . . . today."
–Unknown

share your find

#wonderhunt

fellow wonderhunter

"I noticed this breathtaking sunset from the inside looking out! I was awestruck by the gorgeous colors and how the beveled glass window made it even more amazing! It was definitely a day brightener at the end of the day!" –Dorothy Vesperman

photo tip
You may have heard about the eye-catching Bokeh Effect, taken from the Japanese word for *blur*. Bokeh isn't just a blurred background but also blurred lights. This dreamy technique is fun to use when the background doesn't need to be in focus and you want to draw the eye to the subject in an artful way. Tap your screen to lock in the focus on the subject, then play around with the lighting and the distance between the subject and the light source for varying results.

wonder workout!
Make a "want to do" list this week of things that you don't have to do, but rather want to do. Make an effort to check each item off as you go, celebrating baby steps of progress.

i wonder...
What tools do you utilize when you need help getting unstuck?

SURPRISE ME

Photograph something that represents a surprise you've received.

I'm a huge fan of sunshine. Who isn't, right? I savor sunrises on the horizon; they fill my heart with joy. In the story of our move to Lake Michigan, I learned that one of God's favorite words is "surprise." Our adventurous journey to this house included a handful of unexpected events. And the surprises keep coming, most recently in the form of the majestic moonrise over the lake. Who knew the moon would capture my heart with such intensity? Next time you're looking for wonder, start by saying, "Surprise me!" This invitation allows us to see new discoveries we might have missed.

"Inspiration brings the best out of us. It plays a critical role in our lives. It can be the difference between feeling fully alive and the drudgery of slogging your way through another day. What inspires you?" Matthew Kelly

share your find

#wonderhunt

fellow wonderhunter

"I often ask the Universe to help me when I'm stuck. Such was the case for this challenge. I had no idea what to do, so with my arms open wide, I looked up and said, 'Please, surprise me.' A day or two went by. Then, I looked out my window early one February morning and saw a beach ball in my front yard! A beach ball! In February. In an Illinois town situated in the middle of corn and bean fields. How on earth did a beach ball find its way to my front yard when the nearest beach is a hundred miles away? This challenge reinforced my belief that the Universe can always be counted on. Small and large miracles await us every day. We just need to ask for and then look for them." –Angela Dunlap

photo tip
Create drama and emotion by highlighting the contrasts between extreme lights and darks in your photo. By limiting the visual element through darkness, your mind is left to imagine what's missing, creating intrigue, mystery, and curiosity.

wonder workout!
Watch the film Jason created, which tells the remarkable story of the journey to our big dream, our Sheboygan Surprise, illustrated by his "Here Comes the Sun" series of artwork: https://escapeadulthood.com/sun.

i wonder...
What is a delightful surprise you've received that continues to cause you to shake your head in disbelief?

GRAY VS. GREEN

Take a picture of something old and new in the same shot.

My maternal grandma lived to age ninety-five and was known for her spunky spirit. At her funeral it felt like she had lived two lifetimes. Seeing all of the people she'd played a part in bringing into the world, and her impact on them, displayed to me an undeniable legacy of significance. It reminds me of these awe-inspiring trees in our backyard.

The number of years we will each receive remains unknown, so we need to act accordingly, approaching each day with the delicate newness of a bubble. Delight in playfulness, and stay present in the moment. Your childlike appreciation for each new day will leave a lasting legacy.

> *"Inspiration is perishable."*
> –Scott W. Bradley

share your find

#wonderhunt

fellow wonderhunter

"I love God's gift to me: a little grandson! I'm wonderfully made (vintage, with white hair to prove it). My grandson is three months young and is wonderfully made too. Oh, the places we will go! I'm eager to help him find the beauty we were created to enjoy. Thank you, God, for this precious gift! Please give me energy to keep up with him." –Cathy Rose Monaghan

photo tip
The foreground is the part of the subject in a photo that is closest to the camera. When taking a landscape photo, instead of trying to capture the big picture, put emphasis on something specific in the foreground in order to make for a more interesting shot. This also adds depth to the photo. Move closer to the prominent foreground object in order to bring it into focus.

wonder workout!
Write yourself a letter from your ninety-nine-year-old self. What advise does he/she have you for you today? Are you on the right track?

i wonder...
What's one way you can appreciate something old and new simultaneously in an effort to keep your younger self alive and well?

OBJECT OF MY AFFECTION

Highlight an unusual object that's significant to you, but not to anyone else.

Many times throughout the pandemic, I found my heart fatigue was off the charts. My emotions were so wonky all of the time. I was exhausted from all the feels. I was disappointed to find I could no longer find hearts in nature like I had before. In an effort to stack the deck, I decided to make pipe cleaner hearts and leave them along the paths for others (and myself) to find.

Some seasons require us to make our own magic. Persist in your efforts to find and be the light for others. Your heart is worth fighting for!

> *"God expects something from each of us that no one else can do. If we don't, it will not be done."*
> –Dorothy Day

share your find

#wonderhunt

fellow wonderhunter

"Grandma K had a buckeye tree in her backyard. I love the memories of that childhood garden of Eden: the strawberry patch where I learned that fresh-picked berries taste like love and sunshine; a cherry tree that started me on a lifelong love affair with cherry pie; and a rickety swing set that doubled as a spaceship. I am reminded of my grandma and her singsong voice, her approving smile, and the way she celebrated my creativity. This ordinary seed is a time capsule of wonder from my past and a tiny reminder to hunt for more in my present!" –Jason Kotecki

photo tip
Most of the photos you've take so far have been discoveries of wonder, not staged photos. This one is different however. Have fun putting your selected subject in a setting that highlights contrasts in color, texture or lighting, allowing it to stand out as the hero of the shot.

wonder workout!
This fight against Adultitis is a daily battle. Make sure you are surrounding yourself with friends who support your efforts. Our Escape Adulthood League is a great place to visit and boost your efforts: www.escapeadulthood.me

i wonder...
What object can you put in your line of sight each day to help bring you more joy?

29 FRIENDLY NEIGHBORHOOD ANIMALS

Find a furry, feathery, or funny friend to take a picture of and name.

Just like with Suzy the wren, I love naming our neighborhood animals. Lady the Turkey watched (stalked) us for a while, which brought our family lots of giggles. Then there was Buddy the Deer. Oh, sweet old Buddy; he had some challenges. We also enjoyed ongoing visits from Bethany the Bird, a sweet mourning dove.

This playfulness is an easy win amidst the persisting storm of stress that can often feel out of our control. It's childlike to befriend yard animals, fondly calling them by their "new" names. Channel your inner Snow White and delight in this yard friend whimsy.

> *"A joyful heart is good medicine.*
> *–Proverbs 17:22*

share your find

#wonderhunt

fellow wonderhunter

"I would like to introduce Sebastian. He was not afraid as I approached, and he welcomed me to photograph him while he was dining. Though a graceful animal indeed, he needs to learn some table manners and not drool during his meal. #sometimesweneedrules" –Carolyn Straight

photo tip
When trying to photograph wildlife, intentionality with your timing is key. Nocturnal animals, like owls and opossums, are most easily found during the middle of the day. Birds and deer are quite active at dawn and dusk. It's also a good opportunity to use your zoom settings and practice having a steady hand. Be prepared to be patient and still. Have fun with the process, and enjoy the extra quiet time in nature as you wait.

wonder workout!
Consider a whimsical companion, something simple like a fluffy stuffed animal, a goldfish, or a hermit crab. Adding this friend may present new opportunities for playfulness.

i wonder...
Did you have an animal friend growing up? If so, what fond memories do you recall?

30

WATCH OUT

Reveal a shadow that tells a story.

As I stood on the water's edge, taking in the beauty of the Great Lake as far as my eyes could see, I noticed "she" was alongside me. There's always someone watching, waiting to see if you will lead, and wondering if they should follow. Where will you take them?

It seems safer to stay put, secure and dry in your predictable place. But it's dangerous to play small. Do not hide in your inaction. You will miss out on joy. It is not the time to go into the world gently. It's time to jump in with both feet and let others follow.

> *"Find out who you are and do it on purpose."*
> –Dolly Parton

share your find

#wonderhunt

fellow wonderhunter

"Giddy-up! Where shall we go today? Shall we take the road less traveled and stop without passing a single farmhouse? It doesn't matter to me so long as we go together. I immediately knew I wanted to do this challenge with my horse. I've always loved a good horse story. It was so fun to try different silhouettes and look for ways to play with the light and shadow while working to make sure the horse's shadow looked like a horse and not a big blob or, even worse, a cow." –Martha Henderson

photo tip
Allow the shadow of an object or person to become the central focus in a photo. Look for subject matters with crisp edges to highlight and a clean background to stand out even more. Avoid midday light with the sun overhead; instead, create a scene in which you have only one light source. Have fun experimenting with angles of the camera and movement of the subject.

wonder workout!
Spend some time thinking about who you are leading and who you are following? Is it intentional or accidental?

i wonder...
What joy is waiting for you if you take a leap into the unknown?

31

HOPEFUL HEALING

Take a picture of your favorite place of healing.

This is what we call our "healing swing." It is a place of deep, soulful healing for those open to receiving it.

Living and loving involves hurt and loss. It's not a defeat to need healing; it's simply a part of life. Our heads and hearts carry a lot of disappointment and doubt, shame and regret (and more). This heaviness creates a distance between our mind and our spirit. The farther apart they travel, the heavier and harder life becomes. Taking time to heal frees new space in your mind, and this freedom is a key to unlocking your heart.

> *"Are you ready to not recognize yourself to become who you really are?"*
> —Danielle LaPorte

share your find

#wonderhunt

fellow wonderhunter

"When the pandemic hit, I created an 'office' at my dining room table. Because it was only going to be a few weeks, right? After several months, I decided to convert one of our rooms into my office and make it my own. I wanted to create a special place and surround myself with inspiration. When I'm having a stressful day, I can look in every direction and remind myself of the good that surrounds me. That there is 'hope in the darkness' and so much to be grateful for. I also wanted to create a place where I could step away and just breathe. This photo is a small offering of what is in my 'she den.' It is full of wonder and whimsy."
–Kristen Chang

photo tip

If you want to have big wins with your shots, be intentional about shooting during magic hour (the hour right before and after sunrise and sunset). The soft and hazy light naturally reveals warm colors of gold, pink and blue, creating dreamy photos every single time. Celebrate this time of day by shooting a ton of subjects and savoring the incredible lighting that you simply cannot replicate any other time of day. As a way to put a cherry on top of all of this Wonderhunt photo fun, grab a selfie that represents this experience for you. The golden light will amplify your natural beauty, allowing you to shine bright on a whole new level from the inside out.

wonder workout!

Write a letter to yourself about this Wonderhunt journey. What has surprised you? What would you like to take with you going forward?

i wonder...

Is there a place you go for healing? How often do you make this a priority?

CONCLUSION PART ONE

Hello, Happy Place

Wonder caught me by surprise and continues to. I love to share the stories of how the surprises unfold and I delight in the treasures of these discoveries. Early on in my journey, I wrote this in my journal, reflecting on the gift of Wonderhunt in my life:

> *I was in a rut, missing something.*
> *I had been missing the gift of wonder.*
> *Wonder helped me see with new eyes.*
> *Beauty brought me a flame in my heart, a scavenger hunt for my soul.*
> *In these walks in the woods, I was slowly coming back to life.*
> *Breathing deeper. Savoring my thoughts.*
> *Getting new passions and dreams.*
> *I hadn't realized how far away from these things I had gotten.*
> *I had been missing wonder.*

A friend texted me this Bible verse the other day:

"Come to me, all of you who are weary and carry heavy burdens, and I will give you rest. Take my yoke upon you. Let me teach you, because I am humble and gentle at heart, and you will find rest for your souls. For my yoke is easy to bear, and the burden I give you is light." —Matthew 11:28–30 (NLT)

I had been weighed down by the burdens of my season. I was weary. Wonderhunt brought me to a place of hope and rest. My cup is full (and overflowing) again. Joy and peace are now regular companions on my journey. God is speaking, and I am listening—and noticing.

Last summer I was invited into a new Wonderhunt journey. After twenty-five-plus years, our dream of moving to a lake surrounded by tall pine trees came true. It is our happy place. I longed to savor my newfound opportunity to watch the sunrise over Lake Michigan each day from our magical yard. I decided to "Rise & Shine" (the title of my quest) for thirty days in a row. Experiencing these consecutive sunrises had a significant impact on me.

My prayer throughout the quest was simple. I would sit in our healing swing on the edge of the water and say, "I'm listening." Without fail, every day I would receive the same answer back: "What do you notice?" This question asked of me inspired a journal full of answers. I made a daily practice of noticing, and it

was powerful. On one of the final days of the quest, I received a monumental insight that I'm excited to share with you at the end of this book.

The right question has the ability to change everything. I'm blessed to be married to a guy who is known for asking good questions. The answers often unlock truth and wisdom that guide our next steps.

My daughter, Virginia Rose, presented me with a profound question recently when we were talking about the faith journey in preparation for her First Communion. Point blank she asked, "Mom, what's your cross to carry?"

Wowza! What a question from an eight-year-old. Honestly, it's not a big surprise from her. The well of her heart runs deep. As I mustered up the right words to begin some sort of answer that might be helpful to her (and me), I asked her this question to buy myself time: "What do you think it is?"

"Helping people have a better life," she replied without hesitation.

Her answer filled my heart with joy!

I shared with her the Bible verse that illustrates this for me: "Blessed are the poor in spirit, for theirs is the kingdom of heaven" (Matthew 5:3). Whenever I read this, my heart is consumed with passion because I know it is an invitation from God to help. This verse summarizes my journey of rediscovering wonder and what it means to encourage others to do the same.

We all find ourselves in seasons in which we are "poor in spirit" and the weariness of life weighs on our hearts. I hope the process of learning to Wonderhunt has lightened your load in some way and will continue to as your seasons change and evolve going forward.

Just as Suzy the wren served my childhood self as a guide to wonder in my happy place on that wooden swing, I was gifted another metaphorical Sherpa years later in my new happy place in those woods by our house. She was an old, dying tree, standing on the edge of my well-traveled walking path. She reminded me of a giant sewing needle, inspiring her name: One-Eye.

I loved her, so much so that I told Jason and the kids about her and eventually brought them out to see her. As the kids spent more time with me walking in the woods, we'd make a point to visit One-Eye and enjoy her ever-changing beauty.

These walks had become a special time for me, and the woods and marsh were a place of healing and hope for my weary soul. As I'd get closer to One-Eye's location, I noticed myself appreciating the childlike gift of anticipation. When I'd see her, I'd smile and say hello, savoring the joy she brought me. Silly, I know, but the playfulness served my heart well in that season.

One-Eye taught me about delight, as I noticed new surprises each time I visited. Her colors would change in the varying light at different times of day, and her makeup constantly evolved with the elements. She spoke to my soul deeply about change, aging, and even death as I anticipated what was next for her. There was grace in the process I was witnessing. Her slow decay felt meaningful.

The metaphors of her progression hit me hard some days. It challenged me to ask, "What changes are taking place within me? What is necessarily dying within me? "What lessons am I learning? What do I need to share with others?"

One day, I was shocked to find that though I had been looking at her day after day, I had never noticed the heart that existed on one side of her trunk. What? Had it been there all along? Was it new? Either way, I received it as a small message that she enjoyed my visits just as much as I did. (See it for yourself on page 118.)

Over the years, One-Eye lost strength, and her frame grew smaller. My heart was sad, but I was witnessing a natural process that was both powerful and beautiful. Her eloquent transformation inspired me to think less about loss and more about what would follow—new beginnings.

Then one day it happened. Just a few weeks into the lockdown for the pandemic, as we were wrapping our heads around our new realities and the

weight of the world seemed heavier than ever, I found myself drawn to my Wonderhunts as a safe haven.

As if perfectly timed in this story, I came upon One-Eye and she was on the ground.

I wasn't quite ready for it, and tears came easily. The timing and the symbolism of this was met face-to-face with the collective loss and unending uncertainties of the spring of 2020.

Here's a link to a video of me that day describing the discovery of One-Eye's fall.

Turns out, she had saved her best lesson for after she had fallen.

One-Eye's death was not the end. As the days and months passed, I would walk past her and notice that her structure was breaking apart little by little every day. Her bark was becoming one with the soil, serving the plants and trees around her with nutrients for their own rebirth. New growth and wonder erupted where she lay. Her journey was not over; it had simply changed.

Beautiful even in death. More wonder!

CONCLUSION PART TWO

Goodbye, Happy Place

This book had a surprising ending for me. The manuscript edits were done and already handed to Jason for design and layout. What a great feeling!

But an unexpected evening changed our reality, and the power of Wonderhunt revealed itself to me on a whole new level.

Jason and I were in the basement on our virtual set, celebrating our ninety-ninth episode of Escape Adulthood LIVE, our online show that was born in the pandemic. Broadcasting to our fellow Adultitis Fighters, we were dressed up in full senior citizen costuming. Jason did a kick-butt job on our makeup. He was the cutest ninety-nine-year-old man I had ever seen, with his bushy eyebrows, suspenders, bowtie, and pipe. I was wearing a classic gray-and-silver curly wig, tiny gold glasses on the end of my nose, and white pearls. It was all part of our show's special-edtion shenanigans. We were in our zone with our people.

Early in the livestream there were a few comments about a storm rolling through Wisconsin, but it was hard to determine the weather from our secluded set downstairs. With about twenty minutes of the show remaining, the power suddenly went out. The feed disconnected, and we were plunged into darkness. The flashlight on my phone guided my way as I ran upstairs, knowing that the kids would be freaked out.

As I opened the basement door, they were running towards me in the dark. I couldn't see their faces, but I heard Lucy yell, "Look at the trees!" I was unprepared for what I saw with my quick glance out the kitchen window. It was something out of a nightmare: there were gaping holes where trees used to be, and the ones still standing were sideways.

We all ran into the basement and huddled together praying "Hail Marys." Tight hugs somehow helped us feel more safe in the trauma. And then, as fast as the storm came, it was gone. *What just happened?!*

Later we'd learn that a one hundred per hour straight-line wind had ripped through the north side of Sheboygan. Ours was among the many homes to get hit hard.

Jason went upstairs (yes, still in his costume) to check things out. The sound of his intentional footsteps above us haunted my heart. It was bad, I knew it. My thoughts went straight to his studio. We had been in the middle of adding

Jason's dream art studio to the back of our home. *Was it still there?* It had been such a long and arduous journey to get this far. I knew it would be devastating if it were damaged, or worse.

While we waited for his return, I started prepping the kids, and myself, for loss. "No matter what has happened upstairs, we are safe and have been protected. We can replace things. Stuff doesn't matter. It only matters that we are all okay."

Jason came down to report what he had just seen. The look on his face is one that I will remember forever, one I've never seen from him in our twenty-seven years together, and I hope never to see again. It was a mix of shock, devastation, and dread (knowing the news would break out hearts).

The first thing he said was, "Well, at least 75 percent of the trees in our backyard are gone. There's a tree on the front of our house and at least one on the back of the house. Our driveway is filled with trees, including one on top of our car. There are trees uprooted and thrown everywhere."

It was unreal. Jason and I went upstairs together and walked around like zombies in a horror film. Eerie lightning flickered every few seconds, amplifying our terrifying view. I tried to process the reality that our happy place had changed, never to be the same. Almost all of the trees in our backyard were destroyed, as if someone put them in a giant blender and turned it on.

How could sixty short seconds do so much damage?

We rushed into Jason's new art studio, holding our breath as we turned the doorknob. By the grace of God, it was untouched; not a single scratch. The windows, the skylights, all protected.

Our family's safety, the protection of our home and new art studio, were among the many miracles we would count as the days unfolded.

The hours ahead were filled with the stages of grief well-documented in psychology textbooks. Our backyard, our happy place, my beautiful source of peace and joy, and my once favorite place to Wonderhunt was now ugly, destroyed, and unsafe. It was horrific.

As early as 5:00 a.m. the next morning, after a single hour of sleep, we were hit hard with many Adultitis-ridden realities, including unburying our car and clearing a path on the driveway so that Jason – who had a speaking engagement in Tennessee – could leave for the airport at 6:30. We were without power for the first twenty-four hours, there were insurance claims (and loopholes) to talk through, and many tree companies were offering a variety of solutions.

Only one word accurately described it all… heartbreaking.

For the first forty-eight hours, I couldn't look at the backyard for very long. The kids and I agreed that it was too painful, too difficult, too raw. Every time I glanced back there, it was like looking at a postcard from a recent trip to hell. I wanted to rip it up, throw it away, and move on. But I couldn't.

After a few days, I found myself in need of healing, and I knew there was only one way to do it. I put on my red boots, inserted my earbuds, and walked into our apocalyptic yard in a desperate attempt to Wonderhunt.

As painful as it was to experience, I knew there was wonder to be found, even amidst the brokenness. My weary heart believed it was true.

Just like I had learned from One-Eye, death and destruction was not the end of the story. There would be another chapter to tell (which became the new final chapter of this book!).

My mornings spent Wonderhunting in my once happy, now unhappy place became quite the healing process for me. Tears fell easily (ugly cries, really) and were cleansing, like a refreshing rain badly needed for growth. My prayer was simple and honest, "Reveal wonder to me beyond what I see."

Healing was happening little by little. It was noticeable. I walked slow and steady, almost as if walking on quicksand that would swallow me up if I weren't careful. Safe and brave, one step at a time.

Once again, my head and heart reconnected in this Wonderhunt process, and new lessons and insights flooded my spirit as reminders of truth. I started asking the powerful and trusty question, "Now that this has happened, what does this make possible?" Answers started bubbling up from the entangled branches.

The view of the horizon was clearer than it had ever been. The sun was shining brighter than ever. What was shallow had been uprooted. What was chaotic would soon be cleared completely.

As a family, we started dreaming big about what our happy place will one day be when it's renewed. We envisioned fruit trees (and pies made from their harvest!), a stone fire pit near the bluff, lots of green grass for baseball games and frisbee. The fearful thoughts began untangling and are constantly being replaced with faith, opportunity, wisdom, gratitude, humility, possibilities, favor, and growth.

It's all here in the Wonderhunt journey. Healing and hope. Again.

Wonderhunt is taking on a deeper meaning, a true "scavenger hunt for this weary soul." I do feel like a scavenger, collecting images of sadness and joy and everything in between.

A clearing is coming, and my heart is opening bigger and wider to it with each new day.

Just as I experienced in that first Wonderhunt walk in the woods I shared at the beginning of this book, in my desperate moment, God has once again used wonder to get my attention.

As I continue to be a witness to this process on my spiritual journey, my prayer is that Wonderhunt helps you, as it has helped me.

Maybe you've had a traumatic storm rip through your life, leaving destruction, hurt, and a big mess to clean up. If you've had a deeply personal loss, please know that you are not alone. There is hope on the horizon. Try transforming your fear into curiosity for what's ahead. Keep an eye out for new possibilities.

So yes, our happy place has changed. Maybe yours has too? Change isn't always bad, but it does take some heavy lifting, faith, and creativity to process and manage.

As I type this our healing swing (from Chapter 31) is standing on the edge of our bluff, where it's been since Jason and Ben built it. Yes, it's a little less tall, pinned under a large pine tree, but it's still standing.

So am I.

And so are you.

I am so grateful for this gift of wonder in my life. And I'm so grateful you have taken this Wonderhunt journey with me.

Just like my time spent with Suzy, the soundtrack of my soul is playing new songs. Since my mornings with One-Eye, I now have an appreciation for the changes that allow for new growth. Processing all of this loss and devastation from our storm has allowed me to truly embrace the healing power of looking for wonder.

Although the demands of our lives will continue to be constant, let's continue to make more room in the margins for Wonderhunting, for our wandering and wondering hearts and heads to reconnect on a regular basis.

Let us stand tall with confidence that we are on the right path with a plan to stay the course. May we embrace our full lives—our joyful haul—with an openness that allows us to welcome the new opportunities and challenges that arise each day with hope, peace, and joy.

Thirty-one Wonderhunt challenges. I pray they served your heart and head well as a scavenger hunt for your soul. Did you find what you were looking for?

I invite you to revisit the challenges again and again. They will have new meaning in different seasons of the year and in new seasons of your life. This intentionality will continue to inspire new passion and purpose in your journey.

Instead of seeking easy, try seeking peace. Lift your head to notice the wonder all around you.

As I referred to earlier, at the end of my "Rise & Shine" quest, I was given this insight that I continue to unpack.

The beauty we witness around us doesn't even begin to compare to the beauty within us.

As you continue your Wonderhunt journey, I pray that this scavenger hunt leads you to the beauty and wonder found in your soul.

Keep shining, fellow Wonderhunter!

ACKNOWLEDGMENTS

What a journey Wonderhunt has taken over the years. It's evolved from my own personal journey, to sharing it with others on social media. Then it became a talk I shared at one of our Escape Adulthood Summits, followed by an online course that we ran a handful of times. This transformed into a card deck and evergreen online community, greeting card line, and now this book. All of this was built from the supportive and kind words of others, little by little. Thank you to all who have shared your encouragement with me over the years on this Wonderhunt adventure! It continues to grow because of you!

I am grateful to my amazing parents, Gary and Joyce Halm, for witnessing your faith and service in unending seasons of weariness. By your powerful example, you continue to show me the source of your strength and how to keep searching for light amidst the darkness.

Thank you to my supportive in-laws, Walt and Linda Kotecki. Knowing you're in our corner, cheering and praying for us, has emboldened our courage and given us an amazing advantage over the years, especially in the valleys.

Thank you to my beautiful children, Lucy, Ben, and Virginia Rose, for your encouragement along my journey back to inspired living. I have loved sharing Wonderhunt with you, and your eagerness for this project and mission has been a gift I will forever treasure in my heart. Thank you for finding the hearts with me on our shared path. Your unending love changes me for the better every day.

To Sue and Jenna, thank you for this unending friendship and your faith in action. This foundation was built with your shared sacrifice and love.

To Rachel, thank you for sharing this Wonderhunt journey so personally from the beginning. I am grateful it brought you into this EA world and for our now shared adventure. Your behind-the-scenes efforts on this book have been such a gift.

Special thanks to Jenna Love-Schrader for helping to make this book all that it could be. Your insights in the editing process have been a wonder-full gift!

To my fellow Wonderhunters, many whom contributed to this book with your heart-felt shares, thank you for trusting me on this journey of wonder. I love walking this path with each of you, hearing your insights and seeing the inspiring photos from your own Wonderhunts. I pray this book is a blessing and encouragement to you!

To my talented best friend and husband, Jason. Your encouragement blows me away and lifts me up. I love sharing this adventure with you. Thank you for pushing me out the door and into those woods day after day so many years ago. Thank you for supporting me, one step at a time, throughout this entire process and seeing the Wonderhunt vision even before I could. Somehow, you have convinced me that I am an artist, which is the most encouraging gift to me, inspiring me to write this book. Thank you for bringing this book to life with your thoughtfully inspired design and artistry. I love co-creating with you!

Saving the best for last, I am grateful to God, for not giving up on me! Thank you for your unending grace and mercy on my walk through this life. You are my everything. I pray that you use this book for YOUR glory.

SPECIAL THANKS TO

Katie Bischoff • John Bohannon • Julie Brown • Kristen Chang • Mike & Michelle Clark
Elizabeth Corinth • Rachel Crimmins • Jennifer de Ridder • Mike & Karen Domitrz
Mary Eickemeyer • DeEtte Gastel • Penny Gralewski • Debbie Green • Laurie Guest
Corinne & Bob Hanson • Nic Hawley • Elizabeth Hayson • Martha & Rich Henderson
Jason & Tami Hewlett • Jody Jensen & Tom Plummer • Phil Jones • Heidi Kahlstorf
Brenda Kinnear • Walt & Linda Kotecki • Rebecca Kordatzky • Kathy & Gil Korthals
Victoria Labovsky • Marilyn Loveland • Patricia Maurer • Joe Mull • Musical Pathways
Foundation • Katie Nagle • The National Speakers Association • Amy Payne • Oscar and
Jennifer Pinto • Jenna Regis • Mary Reich • John Reitz • Gail Richardson • Kim Stanfill-
McMillan • Pete & Cheryl Nehnevajsa • Phyllis Thode • Dave Timmerman • Cara & Paul
Tracy • Joyce Trompeter • Kathy Jo Uecker • Mary Beth Updike • Dorothy Vesperman
Betty Vogt • Amanda Ward Prince • Jackie & John Ward • Corey & Joe Wollin

Kim Kotecki is a former kindergarten teacher turned author, artist, and speaker who loves tinkering with photography, capturing the wonder and whimsy of life around her. Since 2000, Kim and her husband, Jason, have worked hand in hand to build their company, Escape Adulthood, a lifestyle brand that inspires Adultitis Fighters to create lives filled with adventure, meaning, and joy.

Kim enjoys her flexible lifestyle, working and playing from home, traveling, and homeschooling her three kiddos. She loves her shared shenanigans as one of the leaders of the Wonder & Whimsy Society—a secret society for people who honor their childlike spirit.

She lives in Sheboygan, Wisconsin, where she enjoys watching the sun rise over beautiful Lake Michigan from her backyard swing, happily eating way too many cheese curds.

fellow wonderhunters

Amy Payne

Colette Matejcak

Wendy Reichel

Martha Henderson

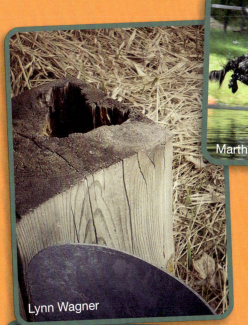
Lynn Wagner

Kim Stanfill-McMillan

Ashley Beranek

Carolyn Straight

Theresa Hamari

Corinne Lenz

Krista Sobieski